P R A I S E   F O R

REAL CHRISTIANITY

Wilberforce is one of the most neglected heroes of modern history—even most Christians are unfamiliar with this thoughtful and passionate Christian whose biblical worldview and dependence on God's Spirit emboldened him to champion the abolition of slavery. This is a man we need to hear from, and Bob Beltz has made him accessible. This 210-year-old book is as relevant as it is important. With Bob's help, it's soul stirring to sit at the feet of Wilberforce, a man God used to change the world.

RANDY ALCORN
AUTHOR, *HEAVEN* AND *SAFELY HOME*

Talk about finishing well! Just days before his death, Wilberforce's great mission to end slavery in Britain was successfully concluded. Now on the eve of the major motion picture release of *Amazing Grace*, there's a new release of Wilberforce's timeless classic, *Real Christianity,* which has been revised and updated by my friend Bob Beltz, who also worked on the film. What a wonderful Christmas 2006 gift to all of us!

BOB BUFORD
FOUNDER, LEADERSHIP NETWORK
AUTHOR, *HALFTIME* AND *FINISHING WELL*

This is a book I strongly recommend. Bob Beltz has done a superb modern translation of one of the all-time Christian classics. I have read and reread *Real Christianity,* and I find its message as timely today as it was when that great Christian leader, the model for my life, William Wilberforce, wrote it. Don't just get this book—read it.

CHUCK COLSON
FOUNDER AND CHAIRMAN, PRISON FELLOWSHIP

The gap between real faith and cultural Christianity is as wide today as it has been at any time in history, so there is much we can learn from William Wilberforce's stirring—and highly successful—cry for reformation. Bob Beltz has done us a great service in making this best-selling classic accessible again.

OS GUINNESS
AUTHOR, *UNSPEAKABLE: FACING UP TO THE CHALLENGE OF EVIL*

Millions of lives were changed as a result of William Wilberforce's determination to change the society of his day. Two hundred years later, the needs around us are still immense. I hope many people will read this new edition of Wilberforce's classic book and be inspired by his example.

NICKY GUMBEL
AUTHOR, *QUESTIONS OF LIFE* AND *A LIFE WORTH LIVING*

Real Christianity is all about living as Jesus lived and doing what Jesus did. It's a must-read for everyone serious about living all and only for Christ.

WALT KALLESTAD
SENIOR MINISTER, COMMUNITY CHURCH OF JOY
GLENDALE, ARIZONA

Wilberforce has long been a hero to many of us. Now, through *Real Christianity*, we get a better glimpse into his theology, his spirituality and his passion. Bob Beltz's adaptation of Wilberforce's original work will provide a needed challenge to all of us, because we're all constantly tempted to let an on-fire, vibrant, world-changing faith cool to a lukewarm "conventional" Christianity.

BRIAN McLAREN
AUTHOR/ACTIVIST (BRIANMCLAREN.NET)

An historic, culture-transforming book by an evangelical politician who changed the history of the British Empire. This classic is still relevant today.

RONALD J. SIDER
PRESIDENT, EVANGELICALS FOR SOCIAL ACTION

REAL
CHRISTIANITY

A Paraphrase in Modern English of *A Practical View of the Prevailing Religious System of Professed Christians in the Higher and Middle Classes in This Country, Contrasted with Real Christianity.*

Published in 1797.

By William Wilberforce, Esq.
Member of Parliament for the County of York

Revised and Updated by Dr. Bob Beltz

Regal

From Gospel Light
Ventura, California, U.S.A.

PUBLISHED BY REGAL BOOKS
FROM GOSPEL LIGHT
VENTURA, CALIFORNIA, U.S.A.
PRINTED IN THE U.S.A.

Regal Books is a ministry of Gospel Light, a Christian publisher dedicated to serving the local church. We believe God's vision for Gospel Light is to provide church leaders with biblical, user-friendly materials that will help them evangelize, disciple and minister to children, youth and families.

It is our prayer that this Regal book will help you discover biblical truth for your own life and help you meet the needs of others. May God richly bless you.

For a free catalog of resources from Regal Books/Gospel Light, please call your Christian supplier or contact us at 1-800-4-GOSPEL or www.regalbooks.com.

Library of Congress Cataloging-in-Publication Data
Beltz, Bob.
  Real Christianity : a paraphrase in modern English of A practical view of the prevailing religious system of professed Christians, in the higher and middle classes in this country, contrasted with real Christianity, published in 1797 by William Wilberforce, Esq., member of Parliament for the county of York / revised and updated by Bob Beltz.
    p. cm.
  Includes bibliographical references (p.   ).
  ISBN 0-8307-4311-1 (trade paper)
  1. Christianity—Early works to 1800. 2. Great Britain—Church history—18th century. 3. Evangelicalism—Early works to 1800. 4. Vocation—Early works to 1800. I. Wilberforce, William, 1759-1833. Practical view of the prevailing religious system of professed Christians, in the higher and middle classes in this country, contrasted with real Christianity. II. Title.
  BR121.3.B46 2006
  274.1'07—dc22   2006027747

           4   5   6   7   8   9   10   /   10   09   08   07

Rights for publishing this book in other languages are contracted by Gospel Light Worldwide, the international nonprofit ministry of Gospel Light. Gospel Light Worldwide also provides publishing and technical assistance to international publishers dedicated to producing Sunday School and Vacation Bible School curricula and books in the languages of the world. For additional information, visit www.gospellightworldwide.org; write to Gospel Light Worldwide, P.O. Box 3875, Ventura, CA 93006; or send an e-mail to info@gospellightworldwide.org.

Contents

Introduction to This Edition

Dr. Bob Beltz

In the following pages I am going to introduce you to a classic book by one of the most amazing figures in British history. His name was William Wilberforce. Perhaps you are reading this book because you are already familiar with the man but have never read his writings. That was certainly the case in my own experience. Then, several years ago, I had the good fortune of becoming part of the team that began production on the feature-length film *Amazing Grace*, which is based on the life of William Wilberforce. Early in the process of working on this film, I decided to read an abridged version of Wilberforce's classic work on Christian faith.

As you can see from the title page, this was a work written at a time when publishers believed that you should deliver as much information in the title of a book as was humanly possible. In 1797, the year the book was first published, catchy titles were not in vogue. Since that time, I have often seen the title condensed to *A Practical View of Real Christianity*. But the intention of Wilberforce was much more focused: He addressed his work to a particular group of people, living at a particular time and place, embracing a unique religious system, which produced a specific religious experience. Hence, to create an accurate and complete title for his book, Wilberforce himself wrote that his text was intended to be *A Practical View of the Prevailing Religious System of Professed Christians*—not of just any group of professed Christians, but specifically professed

Christians who were to be found *in the Higher and Middle Classes in This Country* (i.e., England in 1797). It was the belief system of this specific group of people that was to be *Contrasted with* what Wilberforce called *Real Christianity*.

Because of the specificity of the book, it is difficult to fully appreciate the work at hand without some knowledge of the author and his times. It is not my intention in this volume to write a biography of Wilberforce. Others much better qualified to do so have already undertaken that task. I refer you to the next section, where a brief biography adapted from Kevin Belmonte's *Hero for Humanity* is included, and the bibliography, also graciously compiled by Mr. Belmonte.

My goal in this book is to "translate" Wilberforce's classic work out of the linguistic style of the late eighteenth century into a book that captures Wilberforce's message for a twenty-first-century audience. Wilberforce purists will cringe, I'm sure. But for those who do, it should be noted that Wilberforce, in his book, recommended doing exactly this with works from previous generations that had become inaccessible to the common man because of language or style. For instance, in chapter 6 of the 1824 edition of *A Practical View,* Wilberforce makes the following remark in reference to the 1707 four-volume set of books by Presbyterian pastor Richard Baxter:

> The 1707 edition of Baxter's *Practical Works* are a treasury of Christian wisdom, and it would be a most valuable service to mankind to revise them, and perhaps to abridge them, so as to render them more suited to the taste of modern readers.

My hope and intention in revising and updating this book is that a new generation of modern readers will discover this wonderful man and the timeless message he delivered.

Before you move on to Wilberforce's own introduction, let me inform you that I worked from the fifteenth edition of the complete text of *A Practical View of Real Christianity*. This edition, printed in London by T. Cadell in 1824, is acknowledged as the last version of the book Wilberforce himself edited. The title page of this edition contains two quotes under its lengthy title. I'll present them here as they appeared on the original page:

> *Search the Scriptures!* ———
> John 5:39.

> *How charming is DIVINE PHILOSOPHY!*
> *Not harsh and crabbed, as dull Fools suppose,*
> *But musical as is Apollo's lute,*
> *And a perpetual feast of nectar'd sweets,*
> *Where no crude surfeit reigns.*
>
> John Milton

Wilberforce knew that his readers would do well to follow John's command in order to reap the rewards implied by Milton. I hope this modern version of Wilberforce's work will have the same effect.

WILLIAM WILBERFORCE:
A MAN FOR ALL SEASONS

Kevin Belmonte

By any measure, William Wilberforce was a most remarkable man and, indeed, he has been described as "the greatest reformer in history."[1] His legacy influenced the lives of kings and presidents and touched the poor and downtrodden in nations throughout the world.

Wilberforce was born in the port city of Hull, England, on August 24, 1759, into a prosperous merchant family that we would today describe as "upper middle class." His family harbored hopes that young William might increase the family fortune or perhaps win an election to a prestigious political post. These hopes were not misplaced. Within months of graduating from St. John's College, Cambridge University in 1780, Wilberforce secured a seat in the House of Commons as a member of Parliament for Hull— just a few days after his twenty-first birthday.

By this time, Wilberforce had become a close friend of William Pitt the Younger, who would become the youngest prime minister in British history. Both young men possessed great political gifts. Wilberforce was witty, lively and intelligent. He had a captivating charm and sang so well that in 1782, the Prince of Wales said he would go anywhere to hear Wilberforce sing. Pitt, himself one of Britain's greatest orators, said Wilberforce had the greatest natural eloquence of any man he ever knew. These gifts enabled Wilberforce to overcome the class prejudice harbored by landed aristocrats (who largely ruled England) against the merchant class. He was a young man on the rise.

Pitt ascended to the premiership in 1783 at the incredible age of 24. Less than six months later, Wilberforce was elected a member of Parliament for the county of Yorkshire—one of the most powerful seats in the House of Commons. Yet Wilberforce's path would take a very different course from Pitt's following his election. Wishing to savor the success he had gained, Wilberforce set out on a tour of Europe with his family and a few invited friends. After several months, he returned in the midst of a spiritual crisis that had grown out of conversations he had with Isaac Milner, one of his traveling companions. Milner, an evangelical Anglican with a gift for winsomely articulating "the intellectual heart of Christianity,"[2] was a Fellow of the Royal Society (Britain's national academy of science) and later the president of Queen's College in Cambridge.

Wilberforce returned to London in the fall of 1785, full of doubts about his future. His conversations with Milner had convinced him of the truth of Christianity, but he did not see how, or if, a Christian could serve God in politics. He was in the midst of what he would later describe as his "Great Change," or his embrace of evangelical Christianity.

Not knowing where else to turn, Wilberforce sought out John Newton, the former slave-ship captain turned Anglican parson whom we remember today as the author of the hymn "Amazing Grace." Wilberforce had known Newton as a boy. But Wilberforce's family, alarmed by his growing attachment to someone they considered a religious fanatic, took him away from Newton's influence and that of the evangelical uncle and aunt with whom Wilberforce had been staying.

Yet the good seed planted in Wilberforce's heart by Newton (and by his uncle and aunt) never completely withered. When Wilberforce needed someone to turn to, he knew that he should seek out Newton. It was an inspired choice.

Newton helped Wilberforce see that God had a special purpose for his life—that he could serve God in politics and make a difference there, just as Daniel and Joseph had done in Old Testament times. By 1787, Wilberforce had taken up the charge for which we remember him today: the fight to abolish the British slave trade. And it was John Newton, the former slave trader, whom God used to help Wilberforce see that he should take this course. A man guilty of crimes against humanity had helped set a friend on the path of service to humanity.

At the same time, Wilberforce had become deeply concerned with fostering moral and cultural renewal in Britain. As he wrote in his diary on October 28, 1787, God had set before him two great objects: the suppression of the slave trade and the work of moral reform. And so, even as Wilberforce waged what would be a 20-year fight to abolish Britain's slave trade, he began scores of philanthropic initiatives. In concert with his fellow evangelicals among the Clapham circle (so called because they lived close to one another in the village of Clapham), he pursued reforms of all kinds.

Wilberforce led or was a member of at least 69 different benevolent societies. He was a founder and contributor to the *Christian Observer*, the *Christianity Today* of his time. He helped to found the Sierra Leone colony for freed slaves, the Royal Society for the Prevention of Cruelty to Animals, hospitals for the poor,

Britain's Royal Institution (dedicated to scientific research), and the National Gallery (of art). He was active in educational reform, prison reform, the promotion of public health initiatives and advocating shorter working hours and improved conditions in factories.

Seeking always to be salt and light within his culture, Wilberforce worked with many people who did not share his Christian worldview. His prison reform work with Jeremy Bentham is one example, and his partnership in the abolition of the slave trade with Charles Fox is another. "It is the true duty of every man to promote the happiness of his fellow creatures to the utmost of his power," Wilberforce believed.[3]

One of the most enduring aspects of Wilberforce's cultural apologetic was the publication of his book *A Practical View of the Prevailing Religious System . . . Contrasted with Real Christianity* in 1797. It became an immediate bestseller and went through five editions in six months. By 1826, 15 editions had been printed in Britain, and 25 editions had been printed in the United States. It was translated into Dutch, French, German, Italian and Spanish.

A Practical View of Real Christianity touched many lives throughout Britain. Edmund Burke, the great political theorist and orator, had it read to him during the last few days of his life. It brought him great comfort, and he sent word to Wilberforce saying that if he lived, he should thank his friend for "having sent such a book into the world."[4] The book was instrumental in the conversions of the Scottish moral philosopher Thomas Chalmers and the eminent agriculturalist and travel writer Arthur Young.

To Wilberforce's contemporaries, *A Practical View of Real Christianity* was a *cri de coeur* ("cry from the heart")—a plea for his fellow Britons to embrace what he called vital, or authentic, Christianity. Unlike the turgid, often tedious tomes published at this time, *A Practical View of Real Christianity* was a winsome and conversational book. It was a declaration of Wilberforce's faith commitment, and as such it not only reflected the influence of Jonathan Edwards and Philip Doddridge but also set forth Wilberforce's vision of the good society. People whose lives had been transformed by the truths of Christianity, Wilberforce believed, could enrich the societies in which they lived. And as his legacy attests, he was correct.

Due to poor health, Wilberforce retired from political life in February 1825, having served his nation for nearly 45 years. Yet his passion to secure the emancipation of slaves throughout Britain's colonies continued unabated. He took part in petition drives, guided the younger politicians (such as Sir Thomas Fowell Buxton and Lord Shaftesbury) who inherited his mantle, and spoke publicly when he could. Three days before he died, he learned that Parliament would pass the legislation abolishing slavery throughout the British Empire.

Among the many distinguished African-Americans whose lives were influenced by Wilberforce were William Wells Brown, Paul Cuffe and Frederick Douglass. Many of America's founding fathers were also influenced by Wilberforce's work, including John Quincy Adams, John Jay, Thomas Jefferson, Rufus King, the Marquis de Lafayette and James Monroe. William Hooper, a signer of the Declaration of Independence, even named his son William Wilberforce Hooper.

Among the literary figures affected by Wilberforce were Thoreau, Emerson and Whittier. Jedidiah Morse (the "father of American geography") counted Wilberforce a friend, as did his son Samuel Morse—an artist and inventor so accomplished that he was known as "the American Leonardo da Vinci." Other luminaries of early American culture whose lives were touched by Wilberforce include Caspar Morris, Lyman Beecher, Harriet Beecher Stowe, William Lloyd Garrison, Edward Everett, Jonathan Edwards, Jr., Timothy Dwight (a president of Yale), William Jay, George Ticknor, Abraham Lincoln, William Buell Sprague, Charles Sumner, William Cabell Rives, E. M. Bounds, Arthur and Lewis Tappan, Henry Ingersoll Bowditch, and the parents of the gifted poet William Wilberforce Lord.

The influence of Wilberforce (and the Clapham circle) is not yet exhausted. Wilberforce University of Ohio, America's oldest African-American college, continues to educate young people in our own day. Democratic and Republican leaders in the House and Senate continue to draw inspiration from Wilberforce's legacy. Prison Fellowship, the Wilberforce Forum and the Trinity Forum groups honor and perpetuate his commitment to cultural renewal. Wilberforce's work has obviously not ended.

Following Wilberforce's retirement in 1825, Robert Southey, Britain's Poet Laureate from 1813 to 1843, paid tribute to his old friend. Southey's words serve equally well as a tribute to Wilberforce's enduring legacy: The House of Commons, Southey wrote, "will not look upon your like again."[5]

Notes

1. Description given in a speech by Dr. Os Guinness, Christian educator, writer and speaker.
2. J. Pollock, *Wilberforce* (London: John Constable, 1977), p. 34.
3. W. Wilberforce, *A Practical View of Christianity*, ed. Kevin Belmonte (Peabody, MA: Hendrickson Publishers, 1996), n.p.
4. Kevin Belmonte, "William Wilberforce: The Making of an Evangelical Reformer" (master's thesis, Gordon-Conwell Theological Seminary, 1995), p. 2.
5. Robert Isaac and Samuel Wilberforce, *The Life of William Wilberforce*, vol. 5 (London: John Murray, 1838), p. 238.

WILBERFORCE'S ORIGINAL
INTRODUCTION

Author's Apology: *What I Am*
Attempting to Accomplish

It has been my desire for several years to write to my country-men on the subject of faith.[1] I have been unable to do so until now because of the demands of my position and my poor health. For a long time I have looked forward to the possibility of some season of less demand that would enable me to devote my whole attention to this task. I had hoped for a time when I would not be interrupted by other business, in order that with undistracted attention I might be able to write in such a way that my work would be worthy of the effort a reader might take to read it. It finally became obvious to me that such a season might never come. Therefore, I have taken what free time I have had to undertake this objective instead of being able to give it the kind of attention for which I had hoped. In light of these circumstances, I apologize for any lack of quality that has resulted from this approach.

Regardless of how you might feel about the quality of the writing, let me assure you that what I have written in these pages has not been approached without great care. The subject addressed is of such importance that I have carefully researched, questioned and repeatedly reflected on all that you will read.

Someone will undoubtedly make the objection that because I am not a theologian, I am not really qualified to address this subject. If I need to defend myself against such an objection, I could point out that other writers have done the same. But instead of doing so, I think it should be enough to point out that all of us have the obligation to do whatever we are able to do to promote the welfare of our fellowman. If you love someone who is ruining his or her life because of faulty thinking and you don't do anything about it because you are afraid of what others might think, it would seem that rather than being loving, you are in fact being heartless.

I would suggest that faith is everyone's business. The advance or decline of faith is so intimately connected to the welfare of a society that it should be of particular interest to a politician. Furthermore, the fact that I am not a member of the clergy might help people be more open to what is said in this book. No one can accuse me of writing what I write because I have been motivated by self-interest or theological prejudice.

Enough apologies and justifications; let me get on with the task at hand. Here is what I am going to attempt to accomplish in writing this book.

I'm not going to attempt to either convince skeptics or answer the questions unbelievers always seem to ask, but rather point out some of the problems with the beliefs and actions of those who already claim to be Christians. I'd like to attempt to contrast what we see in the lives of many, perhaps most, who make this claim with what I understand the Bible teaches about what it means to believe in Christ. I am disturbed when I see the majority of so-called Christians having such little understanding of the real nature of the faith they profess. Faith is a subject of such importance that we should not ignore it because of the distractions or the hectic pace of our lives. Life as we know it, with all its ups and downs, will soon be over. We all will give an accounting to God of how we have lived. Because of this fact, I'm not going to pull any punches in what I write. I hope you will seriously consider what is contained within these pages.

That is all I have to say by way of introduction. If what I write seems too rigid or austere, I would only ask that you check what I have to say against what the Bible teaches. That is the only opinion that counts. If you accept the authority of the Bible, I assume you will agree.

Note
1. Wilberforce used the word "religion" here.

CHAPTER ONE

THE STATE OF CONTEMPORARY CHRISTIANITY

*Cultural Christianity, What the Bible Says,
the Problem of Ignorance*

Before looking at the specific problems posed by what I am from here forward going to call cultural Christianity, I would like to address the problem of the faulty ideas many people have regarding the importance of authentic faith. You might think that if you consider yourself a "good" person and are against "bad" things, your faith is adequate. The fact is, you might not be a Christian at all but simply a moral person. You might understand the Christianity our culture has adopted without understanding what constitutes authentic faith. You might know some of the basic facts about Christianity but have no idea how those facts should apply to your life.

I hope you don't think I am being arrogant or overly harsh on cultural Christians. Look at the facts. Do cultural Christians view Christian faith as important enough to make it a priority when teaching their children what they believe and why they believe it? Or do they place greater emphasis on their children getting a good education than on learning about the things of

God? Would they be embarrassed if their children did not possess the former while basically being indifferent about the latter? If their children have any understanding of Christian faith at all, they probably have acquired it on their own. If the children view themselves as Christians, it is probably not because they have studied the facts and come to a point of intellectual conviction but because their family is Christian, so they believe they must be Christians also.

The problem with this way of thinking is that authentic faith cannot be inherited. When Christianity is viewed in this way, intelligent and energetic young men and women will undoubtedly reach a point where they question the truth of Christianity and, when challenged, will abandon this "inherited" faith that they cannot defend. They might begin to associate with peers who are unbelievers. In this company, they will find themselves unable to intelligently respond to objections to Christianity with which they are confronted. Had they really known what they believe and why they believe it, these kinds of encounters would not shake their faith one bit.

I fear for the future of authentic faith in our country. We live in a time when the common man in our country is thoroughly influenced by the current climate in which the cultural and educational elite propagates an anti-Christian message. We should take a look at what has happened in France and learn a lesson from it.[1] In that country, Christianity has been successfully attacked and marginalized by these same groups because those who professed belief were unable to defend the faith from attack, even though its attackers' arguments were deeply flawed. We should be alarmed that instruction in authentic faith has been neglected, if not altogether eliminated, in our schools and universities.

Is it any wonder then that the spiritual condition of our country is of little concern to those who don't even educate their own children about true Christianity? Their conduct reflects their absence of concern, not only for the state of Christianity in our own country, but also for the need to communicate the message of Christ to those in other parts of the world who have not heard this truth.

Some might say that one's faith is a private matter and should not be spoken of so publicly. They might assert this in public, but what do they really think in their hearts? The fact is, those who say such things usually don't even have a concern for faith in the privacy of their interior lives. If you could see their hearts, you would find no trace of authentic faith. God has no place among the sources of hopes, fears, joys or sorrows in their lives. They might be thankful for their health, success, wealth and possessions, but they give no thought to the possibility that these are all signs of God's provision. If they do give credit to God, it is usually done in some perfunctory way that reveals that their words have no sincerity.

When their conversations get really serious, you will see how little of their Christianity has anything to do with the faith taught by Jesus. Everything becomes subjective. Their conduct is not measured against the standard set by the gospel. They have developed their own philosophies, which they attempt to pawn off as Christian faith.

The big problem in these cases is the fact that these men and women have arrived at their conclusions apart from any study of the Bible. The Bible sits dusty on the shelf. These people are biblically illiterate. Their knowledge of the Bible is that of a child.

What a difference it would be if our system of morality were based on the Bible instead of the standards devised by cultural Christians. It would be interesting to see the response of men and women who have set their behavior based on the latter when they were confronted with the standard set by God in the former. Some writers of our time have attempted to illuminate this paradox. Even though they have pointed out the lack of substance of superficial religion, they often have dealt with the issue as one of inadequate information without addressing the more serious issue of the danger this inadequate faith presents. These are eternal issues. The stakes are high.

You have to wonder what God thinks about all of this. I previously made the observation that one day we will have to give an account of how we have lived and what we have done with what God has given us. Because God is concerned about these issues, surely He will also hold us accountable for our stewardship of all the potential instruction we might have taken advantage of to learn the truths of authentic faith. I have to wonder what God thinks of our voluntary ignorance of these matters.

Understanding Christianity is not something that comes without effort. Almost every example in the natural world teaches us this principle. The very way we must exert effort to enjoy all the good things God has provided illustrates this lesson. No one expects to reach the heights of success in education, the arts, finance or athletics without a great deal of hard work and perseverance. We often use the expression "You have to really want it!" Growing in our faith requires the same. Christianity is based on a revelation from God that is filled with information that the natural mind could never have imagined. The wealth of this knowledge will never be mastered without diligent effort.

Carefully studying the Bible will reveal to us our own ignorance of these things. It will challenge us to reject a superficial understanding of Christianity and impress on us that it is imperative not to simply be religious or moral, but also to master the Bible intellectually, integrate its principles into our lives morally, and put into action what we have learned practically.

The Bible is one of God's greatest gifts to humanity. It tells us of the greatest gift that men and women have longed for throughout the ages and of which the prophets spoke about for centuries. When Jesus finally came, His arrival was hailed by the angelic host with the exclamation, "Glory to God in the highest, and on earth peace to men on whom his favor rests" (Luke 2:14). How can you measure the value of the good news of Christ? It is spoken of in the Bible as light in the darkness, freedom from slavery and life from death. Look at how much the Early Church valued the message. They received it with great joy and overflowing gratitude.

Surely all these things should help us come to terms with the inexpressible value of true faith. The greatest gift of God is often either rejected outright or treated as if it is of little worth. But if we really began to study the Bible, we would be impressed with the proper value of this gift. It seems ludicrous that we have to exhort people to study the Bible. The Bible itself speaks words of challenge to us such as, "Be prepared to give an answer to everyone who asks you to give the reason for the hope that you have" (1 Pet. 3:15). Those who have done so tell us of the immense value of such effort. And yet, though many have the

Bible on the shelf in their homes, for most the content of the Book remains a mystery. The result is that in the Christian world in the West, we settle for a cultural version of Christianity that is far from the real thing.

I'm not talking about unbelievers here. I am speaking of those who say they believe the Bible is the Word of God and who claim to have committed their lives to Jesus Christ. They have given in to a nominal faith. They agree with statements such as, "It doesn't matter what you believe; it is how you live that counts" and "It doesn't matter what you believe, as long as you are sincere in your belief." How absurd!

What we believe determines how we live. Men who sincerely believed that what they were doing was right have perpetrated many of the most hideous crimes against humanity. Again, the recent events in France serve as a clear example of this fact. Almost all people believe they are living good and moral lives. Yet they measure their lives against some subjective criteria without realizing that vice is often the product of ignorance or error. Such people often lack the ability to distinguish right from wrong or truth from error.

This is one reason why the diligent study of the Bible is so important. It is here that God has given us the instruction we need to be able to tell right from wrong and truth from error. Without understanding its principles and precepts, we become victims of our own subjectivity. How profitable is subjectivity if our conscience has been seared, our heart hardened, and our mind blinded to all moral distinctions?

An authentic faith requires an honesty of mind, the consistent use of the means of knowledge and instruction, the humility that fosters a desire to be instructed, and an unprejudiced conclusion about what this inquiry reveals. If we approach the study of the Bible this way, God fulfills His promises. If we seek and keep on seeking, we will find; if we ask and keep on asking, we will receive; if we knock and keep on knocking, the door to truth will be opened. How can we refuse an offer like this?

Yet such opportunity is accompanied by responsibility. If we have settled for cultural Christianity and remained igno- rant or unresponsive to authentic faith, what kind of justifica- tion will we be able to give to God?

Note
1. Wilberforce repeatedly uses France as an example of a sick society. In 1797, when this book was originally written, England was still battling French revolutionary forces that were attempting to conquer Europe. The French Revolution had radi- cally impacted the culture and values of France. Wilberforce uses this as an illus- tration of what could happen in England.

CURRENT IDEAS ABOUT THE NATURE OF MAN

Section One: *Faulty Ideas About the True State of Humanity*

Having looked at the lack of understanding that exists among most cultural Christians about the importance of authentic faith in general, we now will look more specifically at the faulty ideas most Christians have about the true spiritual state of humanity. This is a topic about which many who read this book might not have given much thought. If that is true in your case, I ask you to pay special attention to what follows. This is a subject of extreme importance. The truth about this subject is at the very heart of all authentic faith.

It is my opinion that the majority of Christians overlook, deny or, at the very least, minimize the problems of what it means to be a fallen human being. They might acknowledge that the world has always been filled with vice and wickedness and that human behavior tends toward the sensual and selfish. They might admit that the result of these facts is that in every age we can find innumerable instances of oppression, cruelty, dishonesty, jealousy and violence. They might also admit that we act this way even when we know better.

These facts are true; we don't deny them. They are so obvious that it is a mystery why so many still believe in the goodness of human nature. But even though the facts might be acknowledged, the source of the facts is often still denied.

These things are rationalized as small failures or periodic problems. Other explanations are given that fail to get to the heart of the matter. Human pride refuses to face the truth. Even the majority of professing Christians tend to think that the nature of humanity is basically good and is only thrown off course by the power of temptation. They believe that sin and evil are the exception, not the rule.

The Bible paints a much different picture. The language of Scripture is not for the faint of heart. It teaches that man is an apostate creature, fallen from his original innocence, degraded in his nature, depraved in his thinking, prone toward evil, not good, and impacted by sin to the very core of his being. The fact that we don't want to acknowledge these truths is evidence of their veracity. As Milton said in *Paradise Lost*:

Into what depth thou seest,
From what height fallen![1]

Think about the amazing capabilities of the human mind. We have the power to invent, reason, make judgments, remember the past, make decisions in the present and plan for the future. With the ability to discern, we do not merely understand an object; we can admire it, especially if it reflects something of the beauty of moral excellence. Emotionally, we have the ability to fear and hope, experience joy and sorrow, empathize and love. With the will, we can exercise courage to do hard tasks and exert patience to stay the course. With the power of conscience, we can monitor the thoughts and desires of our hearts and use reason to regulate our passions. We are truly amazing creatures. If aliens from another world observed us, they would be astonished at our ability to use all these faculties to be the best we can be. They would think that our Creator would delight in all the good we would choose to do with these marvelous attributes.

Unfortunately, we all know that this is not the way things are. Take a look at how we actually use these powers. Step back and take a look at the big picture of human history. What do we see? We see that human reason has become confused. Human desires have become twisted. Anger, envy, hatred and revenge rear their ugly heads. We have become slaves to our lower natures and seem unable to do good!

History confirms these tragedies of human nature. Ancient civilizations were not characterized by good. On the contrary, even the most advanced cultures were cloaked in moral darkness. We find superstition, the lack of natural affections, brutal excesses, unfeeling oppression and savage cruelty everywhere we look. Nowhere do we see decency and morality prevail. In the words of Paul, "Therefore God gave them over in the sinful desires of their hearts to sexual impurity for the degrading of their bodies with one another" (Rom. 1:24).

If we change our focus from the ancient to the modern, we find the same condition. One historian described America in the following way:

> It is a compound of pride, and indolence, and selfishness, and cunning, and cruelty; full of a revenge that

nothing could satiate, of a ferocity that nothing could soften; strangers to the most amiable sensibilities of nature. They appear incapable of conjugal affection, or parental fondness, or filial reverence, or social attachments; uniting too with their state of barbarism, many of the vices and weaknesses of polished society. Their horrid treatment of captives taken in war, on whose bodies they feasted, after putting them to death by the most cruel tortures, is so well known, that we may spare the disgusting recital. No commendable qualities relieve this gloomy picture, except fortitude, and perseverance, and zeal for the welfare of their little community, if this last quality, exercised and directed as it was, can be thought deserving of commendation.[2]

Even in the most civilized of nations we see the truth of the fallen nature of humanity. In some of these nations, Christian influence has set the bar much higher than in what we might consider to be pagan nations. Generally, Christian influence in a nation has improved the character and comforts of society, especially in reference to the poor and the weak, who have always been accorded special attention by those professing Christian faith. This influence has created great blessings for many, even though these same people deny the truth of the Bible and do not accept its authority. But, even in those nations that have been influenced by biblical faith, we see many examples of human depravity.

When the true nature of man is revealed in situations where Christian influence once held sway, depravity becomes even more obvious. The laws and conscience of such societies have been designed to restrain these forces of human nature. When these laws are removed or violated, we see the most hideous and atrocious crimes perpetrated shamelessly and in broad daylight.

When you consider the biblical teaching concerning superior morality and obedience to the teachings of Christ combined with the truth that one day we will give account for our actions, it is a marvel that we have made so little progress in virtue. We still exhibit the characteristics attributed to less-informed societies; i.e., prosperity hardens the heart, unlimited power is always abused, bad habits develop naturally, while virtue, if obtained at all, is slow, hard work. Even moralists rarely practice what they preach. It seems the rule that people are more willing to suffer the negative consequences of vice than take advantage of the blessings of living a life of Christian obedience.

If we seek more evidence of the fallen nature of humanity, we need look no further than our own children. Even parents with the strongest Christian principles can testify how baffling it is to attempt to correct our children when they rebel against us in attitude and action.

Another example of the most twisted variety is how we can take the truth of the Bible and use it for the most hideous purposes. Christ gets vilified when those who bear His name use it as an excuse for cruelty or persecution. We must be careful to distinguish twisted zeal from true Christian commitment. History provides too many examples of people who called themselves Christians but were in fact devoid of the love and kindness of Christ. It is as if a healing medicine had become a deadly poison. How tragic that those of us who identify ourselves as followers of Jesus, who have the benefit of the revelation of God's Word, who have been exposed to the truth of the very nature of God, who profess that "in him we live and move and have our being" (Acts 17:28), who acknowledge His provision and blessing in our lives, and who have accepted the forgiveness provided by the death of Christ on the cross, continually forget His authority over our lives and become cold and uncaring about Him in our hearts.[3]

Maybe the best testimony concerning depravity comes from those whose commitment to Christ is wholehearted. They can testify how difficult it is to fight against their fallen nature as they attempt to live lives of obedience. They will tell you that by observing their own lives and the way their minds work, they have discovered how corrupt the human heart really is. Every day this conviction grows. They will tell you of how poorly they are able to live out their convictions, how selfish their desires are, and how feeble and halfhearted are their attempts to do the right thing. They will acknowledge and confess that the biblical teaching about the two conflicting natures has proven true in their experience. In the words of Paul, "I have the desire to do what is good, but I cannot carry it out" (Rom. 7:18). As someone has said, even the spirituality we do possess is corrupted by our nature. We have nothing to brag about. On the contrary, God must always give us grace to bear with our faults and mercy to forgive our sins.

This is the true spiritual condition of humanity. The nuances of particulars and intensity might be different in each individual case, but the underlying principles remain true. Whether ancient times or modern, human history is a record of human depravity. This is the humbling truth.

When we examine the amazing capabilities humans possess and then compare it to what we have done with them, we have a hard time explaining the contrast. It is hard to find rational explanations. The only explanation seems to be that since humanity lost its relationship with God, something has become fundamentally and fatally flawed with every person born on this planet. As a result, even though we have the ability to say no to the lower appetite, it has become strong enough to overpower the inclination to do right.

This tendency has created a resistance in our fallen nature to know the truth about God. We don't want to know that there is a God who places moral restraints and ethical expectations on us. The more we sin, the more fixed this reality becomes. We have been locked in handcuffs of wickedness that keep us from doing good and seeking God. The deeper we sink into this folly, the less we understand of the truth and the harder the heart becomes in its ability to respond to God. Our thinking and faulty consciences are so distorted that they add to the problem by creating delusions of righteousness. Instead of being sick about the true state of our being, we actually think everything is fine with us.

This is the way sin works. It is true that there are greater and lesser degrees of distortion found among people. Some are obviously living in bondage. Others give the appearance that they have overcome such problems. But the fact remains that even if it is not apparent in a person's outward behavior, this is the true state of all our hearts.

This reality is so pervasive that the only explanation for it must rest in some defect in the human condition. This imperfection would appear to be the only explanation that adequately can account for the facts. This is not mere speculation but a demonstrable reality validated in much the same way as Sir Isaac Newton proved his scientific theories through experimentation and observation of the facts. It is the only theory of human nature that fits all the evidence.

At this point, it becomes necessary to turn from pure reason and observation to see what the Bible says about this situation. The Bible resounds with overwhelming statements about the fallen nature of man. On nearly every page of the book we find validation for this doctrine. We read texts such as, "The imagination of man's heart is evil from his youth" (Gen. 8:21, *KJV*). "What is man, that he could be pure, or one born of woman, that he could be righteous?" (Job 15:14). Romans chapter 3 says that all have sinned and gone astray. There is not one righteous person. We could go on and on: "The heart is deceitful above all things and beyond cure. Who can understand it?" (Jer. 17:9). "Surely I was sinful at birth, sinful from the time my mother conceived me" (Ps. 51:5). Like Paul, we should cry out, "What a wretched man I am! Who will rescue me from this body of death?" (Rom. 7:24). No wonder the Bible says that a complete change of nature is required if we are to live the way God intended us to live.

Section Two: *Faulty Ideas About Evil*

As if the picture the Bible paints of the natural state of fallen man is not bad enough, we also need to take into account how demonic activity is at work in the fallen human heart. In the Bible, Satan is called "the prince of this world" (John 12:31). This is one area that immediately distinguishes cultural Christianity from authentic biblical faith. In a nation that claims to believe in the Bible, the doctrine of the existence and activity of the devil is almost universally denied. Some of what the Bible teaches, even if not affirmed, is often tolerated. But the issue of evil personified is another story. It is treated like an old fairy tale. We are given the impression that it is a subject any educated man has ceased to believe; like a superstition that belongs with stories about ghosts, witches and other phantoms that are remnants of a less-enlightened time. It is true that this is a teaching of the Bible that has been horribly distorted. Some wrongly believe that the portrayal of Satan and his minions as ghastly beasts with horns and tails comes from the Bible. Excesses among believers, attributed to these agents, become ammunition to further discredit their reality.

Consequently, this is a subject people either ignore or ridicule. This seems inconsistent considering we acknowledge the reality of wicked men, twisted in their thinking and actions, who often successfully lure their fellow humans into sin and evil. Why then does it seem incredulous that there might exist spiritual beings of like propensities that tempt men to sin? It is only a presupposition of materialists that such beings cannot exist that keeps them from seeing the inconsistency of their position. They simply do not believe what the Bible teaches on this subject.

For those who do believe, this is a serious matter. It makes us realize what a battle we are engaged in. We are flawed within and tempted from without. What hope do we have? When we first read what the Bible says about God, it only makes our condition seem all the more hopeless. We are told that we can't hide anything from God. He knows what we do, and He even knows what we think. He knows what is in our hearts. He sees the inner darkness.

Add to this the things the Bible says about God's judgment and the lessons of His vengeance inflicted upon Israel. From Sodom and Gomorrah to Nineveh and Babylon, we see God judge man's sin. Even though we know something of the goodness of God, the examples we read must surely cause us some measure of apprehension about our own failure to live according to the instructions God has given. What will we do with passages such as these:

> But since you rejected me when I called and no one gave heed when I stretched out my hand, since you ignored all my advice and would not accept my rebuke, I in turn will laugh at your disaster; I will mock when calamity overtakes you—when calamity overtakes you like a storm, when disaster sweeps over you like a whirlwind, when distress and trouble overwhelm you. Then they will call to me but I will not answer; they will look for me but will not find me. Since they hated knowledge and did not choose the fear of the LORD (Prov. 1:24-29).

It is an understatement to observe that this is very serious language. Not that the Bible needs affirmation, but the world around us demonstrates that there is a kind of sowing and reaping that affirms the destructive nature of ignoring the things the Bible teaches. Sin has consequences. We see those consequences all around us.

If all this is true, what can we do? Is there any hope? Is judgment our only destiny? Gratefully, there is hope. When we come to grips with the true state of our condition, we are ready to fully appreciate what God has done to rescue us from ourselves. It is imperative that we take seriously our true condition as fallen human beings. Without this understanding and acknowledgment, we will not have an adequate foundation on which to build an authentic faith. This is not theological babble; it is a practical issue. When we do not take our problem seriously, we do not seek the solution God offers with the measure of sincerity and intensity that our true condition requires. If we don't understand how seriously ill we are, we don't pursue the remedy with the required diligence. If we are slightly ill, we take an aspirin. If we are dying, we passionately pursue a cure. The cure is *not forced on us*; it is *offered to us*.[4]

It is a great advantage to understand how defective we actually are. It helps us shake off false security and nominal spirituality. Only an unwillingness to be open and honest can keep us from the conclusion that both reason and experience tell us that what the Bible says about us is true. We are without excuse if we remain in denial.

Not only should we agree with this intellectually, but we must also feel the truth experientially. When we see around us the tragedy of not taking this truth seriously and when we experience within ourselves the veracity of the truth, we will be positioned to move forward in our spiritual progress. We also will have a different attitude toward those who more obviously struggle in areas where we might only secretly have a problem. Day by day, an awareness of our condition will help us grow spiritually.

Section Three: *Objections to These Facts*

With all that has been said, we still have not faced our biggest problem: Pride does not like to be humbled. When faced with the facts, the proud man attempts to rationalize these things by blaming them on God. After all, the reasoning goes, who created us? The proud man thinks this approach somehow excuses him from the guilt of sin. He thinks that God will not hold him accountable by standards he, by nature, claims he cannot keep. This circular and illogical reasoning makes no sense.

If we explore this reasoning when nonbelievers apply it, we have another story. Even if we show them the flaw in their thinking, it still does not mean that they will be open to the message of the Bible. If we can simply engage these men and women in honest dialogue, we might have a better chance of communicating using the solid arguments in favor of Christian faith that even the most intellectual of skeptics have affirmed. If we can demonstrate adequately the case for Christianity, then the previous mental gymnastics play a small part in their objections.

Start with the basics before you attempt to explain the unfathomable mind of God. It is my opinion that this is the best way to approach those who do not believe. Of course, it is important to remember that I am addressing these pages to those who claim to already embrace Christian faith. For those who acknowledge the goodness and justice of God as well as the fallen nature of man, the latter is never an adequate excuse to explain human sin. We are accountable, not excusable.

The Bible specifically states that sin cannot be blamed on how God made us. "When tempted, no one should say 'God is tempting me'" (Jas. 1:13). God wants us to come to terms with our sin and embrace the solution He has provided that can save us from judgment.

When we excuse our behavior and do it in the name of theology, we effectively set the stage for disaster. We are all accountable: Our fallen nature is no excuse. We are responsible: God is not to blame. We stand guilty and deserving judgment. Any other teaching dilutes and refutes the true significance of the cross of Christ. When you put it together, it looks like this: Our natural condition is weak and fallen and our temptations are numerous; God is infinitely holy, yet He offers forgiveness, grace and enabling power to those who get honest with Him and are willing to repent.

This might not be easy to understand. What in life is? The mysteries of the universe should be enough to remind us of our limitations and create humility within us. Is it any wonder that we can't totally understand the infinite God? And even though some things about the Christian faith are hard to understand, the basic truths are plain and obvious. Some things God has revealed; others remain mysteries. Let's focus on what we do know, not on what we can't understand.

For those of us who have come to know that life is training us for eternity, we have a hard time understanding the person who continues to be consumed by trivial and arrogant curiosity while ignoring the good news of all Jesus Christ has to offer. It is like coming before a judge in the courtroom on a charge you are obviously guilty of committing and then, when the judge offers a way of avoiding punishment, turning around and attempting to blame the judge for what happened. That would be absurd! When we think all this through, we come to appreciate what John Milton wrote:

What better can we do, than prostrate fall
Before him reverent; and there confess

Humbly our faults, and pardon beg; with tears
Watering the ground, and with our sighs the air
Frequenting, sent from hearts contrite, in sign
Of sorrow unfeign'd, and humiliation meek?[5]

Notes

1. John Milton, *Paradise Lost,* bk. 1, lines 91-92.
2. Wilberforce is here quoting William Robertson's *History of America.* It should be remembered that the British were not fond of America at this point in time. In 1797, the year of publication of Wilberforce's book, George Washington was finishing his second term as president and King George III was still on the throne of England. Wilberforce himself had opposed England's opposition against the colonies and was friends with many Americans, including Benjamin Franklin.
3. Wilberforce is here referring to instances in history where great evil has been done in the name of Christ. He may have been thinking of such events as the massacre of innocent women and children during the Crusades or the evil of the Inquisition, where many innocent victims were cruelly tortured and put to death in the name of Christ.
4. Wilberforce italicizes these words in the original manuscript.
5. Milton, *Paradise Lost*, bk. 10, lines 1086-92.

CHAPTER THREE

UNDERSTANDING CULTURAL CHRISTIANITY

Faulty Thinking About Jesus Christ and the Holy Spirit, a Few Comments on the Interaction of Emotions and Faith

Section One: *Essential Truths of Authentic Christianity*

There are certain essential facts about Jesus Christ and the Holy Spirit, which the Bible teaches, and, historically, the Church embraced. They include:

1. God loved the world so much that He sent His only son, Jesus Christ, to redeem us.
2. Jesus Christ willingly left the glory of the Father and became a man.
3. Jesus was despised by many people. He was rejected and experienced sorrow and grief.
4. Jesus suffered because of our sin.
5. Jesus went to the cross and took our sins with Him so that through His death we could have eternal life when we repent of our sin and accept what He has done for us.

6. Jesus rose from the dead and ascended to heaven where He now is in the presence of the Father and intervenes for us.
7. Because of what Jesus has done, we can come into the presence of God with confidence and get the help we need when we are in trouble.
8. God gives the gift of the indwelling Holy Spirit to those who enter into a relationship with Jesus Christ.
9. It is the presence of the Holy Spirit in our lives that makes us true Christians.
10. The influence and activity of the Holy Spirit in our lives works to transform us and make us the kind of people God intended us to be.
11. True believers will be raised from the dead and live forever in God's presence.

These are the basic truths of Christian faith. We will take them as givens. Virtually everyone who goes to church has heard these things repeatedly. However, that does not mean that those who know these things intellectually have a deep understanding of their significance or experience their transforming influence in their lives. The appropriate response to these facts would be one of great excitement, true humility, hatred of sin, humble hope, firm faith, heavenly joy, ardent love and unceasing gratitude!

But here is where we find a problem with the experience of those who hold to a cultural Christianity. It is a defect that is like a cancer that begins as undetectable and ultimately spreads to ravage the entire body. It is not until people are aware they are sick that they recognize their need for a physician. If they do not come to terms with their desperate spiritual condition, they cannot understand the infinite value of what Jesus Christ has done nor respond to it appropriately. Their lives are filled, as Jesus said, with the business and vanities of this life.

These tendencies are harder to detect in those who are a bit more thoughtful about their cultural Christianity. If you want to know how serious these men and women are about Christ, engage them in conversation and steer the discussion toward matters of faith. What do you find? You often find a vague faith. By this I mean that you will receive responses to your questions and comments that are unclear at best.

Cultural Christians might talk about religion or church in generic terms, but you will rarely hear them use the name of Jesus or speak of His death on the cross or His resurrection. If you raise the subject, you might find that they are uncomfortable and don't care to talk about the very thing that thrills the heart of all those who possess authentic faith. They will speak of moral precepts and positive character qualities in the abstract but not as they specifically relate to Jesus. It is as if what Jesus has done for humanity does not connect in their thinking with the fact that it was done specifically for them.

It is our good fortune that these wonderful truths have been written down for us. We recite these truths in our services, even if we hear nothing of them from the pulpit. How can these wonderful things be treated as some kind of ancient history with no bearing on the present moment? How can they be spoken of with so little emotion? We hear of them with indifference and respond to them as if by rote. We leave the church and do not think of them again until the next Sunday. The term "lukewarm," given by Jesus Himself, aptly describes this tepid faith. I hope you do not think I am being too harsh or critical. I am only attempting to describe what I have seen. Again, remember, I am speaking here of those who claim to be Christians! How can these things, so precious to God, be treated with such coldness?

What does it mean to love God? True love is passionate. "Cold love" and "unfelt gratitude" are contradictions. When we love someone, we like to talk about him or her. Such conversations are rarely without emotion. We want to be with them. We delight in doing things for them. We love to show them how we feel. The mention of their name makes our hearts pound and our faces light up.

Authentic faith responds to the work of Jesus Christ in just such a way. A lukewarm disposition toward these things makes us question if the person really understands at all. When faith is lukewarm, or nominal, the exercise of faith cannot be expected to be very vigorous. It is a belief system that has no effect on the way the person lives.

If this were not bad enough, the situation is even worse when it comes to the Holy Spirit. Cultural Christians probably have no understanding of the work of the Spirit in the life of the believer. Since they do not strive for effectiveness in their own spiritual lives or attempt to live with character consistent with followers of Christ, they have no experience of their own inability to achieve such things without the Holy Spirit's help. As such, they do not take advantage of the disciplines required on a regular basis to keep the work of the Spirit active in their lives. Their understanding of the facts is so shaky and confused that it could be said that they really don't believe in the Holy Spirit at all.

There are those who suggest that whenever you see true spiritual passion, you also find hypocrisy and delusion. Some might even say that talk about a love for Jesus is the sign of a sick mind. They argue that true religion is sober and steady, that it is not a matter of feeling or enthusiasm. They will point out that emotions are subjective and unreliable.

The typical objection against an emphasis on the Holy Spirit will raise the issue of false manifestations of spiritual experience and the abuse such actions have produced. Those who make the objection will talk of hypocrites and fanatics and point out that from time to time the same claims and exaggerated stories have circulated. They will argue that any emphasis on depending on the work of the Holy Spirit removes personal responsibility and leads to laziness. Because of this, they advocate focusing on that which is more "solid" and "practical." Cultivating the virtues of a moral character becomes the focus of their religion, instead of commitment to Jesus Christ.

In its most vehement form, this argument goes so far as to attribute the atrocities of the Crusades, the Inquisition, and the conquest and exploitation of native populations to those who were overly enthusiastic in their practice of Christianity. This is a great misunderstanding of authentic faith. This equates zeal with authentic faith. Authentic faith will often be accompanied by an appropriate zeal. But zeal can often be devoid of any accurate understanding of authentic faith. The product of such zeal is often justified in the name of Christianity, but in reality it has virtually nothing to do with believing in Jesus Christ.

The truth is that those who most closely follow the teachings of Christ are the first to admit that Christianity has been horribly guilty of all these things. However, it is not the faithful follower of Christ who is responsible but rather those who have twisted the Bible to fit their own agendas that are guilty of such actions. People who follow Christ faithfully are also the first to acknowledge that the teaching on the person of the Holy Spirit and His activities has been used to justify some of the most bizarre actions in the history of Christendom.

We must remember that almost any ideology can be distorted and misused to bring misery to multitudes or justification to the most bizarre behavior. Nothing is more dangerous. That which is intended to motivate goodness and restrain evil actually can become the instrument of that which it intended to restrain. History is full of examples of how virtues such as liberty or patriotism become twisted when separated from a healthy and authentic faith. Twisted men in every generation and occupation have twisted whatever they must twist to get what they want. Why should we expect that some within the Church would not be guilty of the same actions?

In cases in which excess has become a part of the religious culture, we need to look beyond the surface behavior to the motivation that lies underneath. The educated person might find the faith of the uneducated somehow offensive to his "good taste." But were he or she to take time to get to know the uneducated believer, that person might discover a purity of heart that puts his or her own to shame. In many cases, what you will find in those who avail themselves of the Spirit's activities in the human heart is love of Christ, ardent and active zeal in His service, prudence, meekness, courage and a quiet consistency. Such behavior needs no argument to defend.

Section Two: *Emotions and Faith*

In light of the above, what is the role of emotions in authentic faith? If our relationship with Jesus Christ involves an emotional response, does that mean we have abandoned rational thinking? Critics of emotional faith must either believe that religious emotion is always unreasonable or that faith is not an area where emotion should play a role. Surely they cannot believe that emotion in and of itself is always unreasonable. Since educated people who understand the operation of the mind know this is not the case, it seems we must look at the possibility that it is in the religious sphere—and specifically in relation to Jesus Christ—that emotion does not belong.

It appears that the idea that religion is not a place for emotion is a prevailing attitude in our culture today. It is believed that emotions that are not held in check with regard to issues of faith lead to excess. Part of the reason for this kind of thinking is that a healthy emotional response to faith, one that is warm and affectionate, has almost ceased to exist and has been replaced by one that is predominantly a matter of the head and not of the heart. Certainly, part of the problem is a misunderstanding of the role of healthy emotions in regard to faith. It is as if we have been told we need to amputate one of our legs without getting a second opinion about other options. I hope you will indulge me a bit more, because this is an issue that has not adequately been addressed.

Men and women are emotional beings. It is a major part of who we are. So how can emotions not play a role in our faith?

It would seem that God has created us with this capacity so that it can play a role.

What to do with our emotions has been the subject of philosophers throughout the ages. Philosophical thought seems to come down to two theories on what to do with emotions. On the one hand, there are those systems of philosophy that attempt to create rules to control emotion so that it does not get out of hand. On the other hand are systems that advocate putting emotions to death totally, i.e., exterminating them! This would be the equivalent of exterminating an entire race that you have conquered and then calling what you have done peace. As the ancient historian and philosopher Tacitus observed:

> To plunder, butcher, steal, these things they misname empire: they make a desolation and they call it peace.[1]

Authentic faith does not need to approach the issue in either way. Only those who have such faith understand that part of the beauty of Christianity is that it integrates all the dimensions of true humanity, bringing appropriate subordination and dependence so that the whole man, using all his faculties, can be transformed by the power of God in such a way that all of who he is can be used to the service and glory of God. God wants our hearts as well as our minds. Jesus said that we are to love God with all our heart (see Matt. 22:37). Certainly even a casual reading of the Bible shows men and women whose emotions played a central role in their relationship with God. If you doubt what I say, read the Bible! God desires that we relate to Him with love, warmth, tenderness and zeal. He hates lukewarm religion, the very thing some current clergy advocate.

Real worship taps into and uses the emotions. Music, singing, praise and rejoicing—they all need emotion to be authentic. This certainly was the case with people in the Bible. They were warm, zealous and affectionate. When engaged in worship, their souls seemed to become ignited with rapture. It would be hard to study the life of the apostle Paul and not see the measure of emotion that was involved in all he did and all he wrote. Read the psalms. David was a man who experienced great emotion in his faith. He knew the heights and he knew the depths. Remember that he is called "a man after [God's] own heart" (Acts 13:22). Even the pictures we are given of life in heaven are filled with great emotional response.

This is not to suggest that an emotional response is the measure of authentic faith. That would be the opposite error. Any good actor can conjure up almost any degree of emotion. Also, individual temperament can play a major role in how much emotion is attached to our faith. Emotions must be judged by what arouses them.

One way of assessing valid emotion in relationship to faith is to look at the object that has stimulated the emotion. A good orator can whip a crowd, even a Christian crowd, into a frenzy. This is not the kind of emotion that God desires. When emotion is a response to truth or to a clear comprehension of the nature of God and His goodness to us, then emotion is valuable and appropriate.

Perhaps the most important question in evaluating religious emotion is whether it is an end in itself or a source of motivation to put faith into practice. Any other means of evaluation can become subjective, but what conduct our emotion produces can be clearly measured.

True love is not simply an emotional response. It manifests itself in acts of kindness, generosity and those actions that produce the greatest benefit to the object loved. Therefore, as Jesus said, "Whoever has my commandments and obeys them, he is the one who loves me" (John 14:21). How are we doing? This is the true test of the value of emotion.

I do acknowledge that emotional response is found in different degrees in different people. Temperament certainly plays a role. A person who is warm and animated in normal life will generally be the same about his or her faith. That is, unless normal behavior is repressed to meet some set of imposed criteria. On the other hand, a person who tends to be cold and unemotional in daily life can hardly be expected to have an emotion-filled faith.

Emotions not only play a large role in faith, but they also must be controlled in order that we do not let emotions lead to actions that harm our growth in authentic faith. Like Paul, the poet Ovid confessed:

I see the better and approve it, but I follow the worse.[2]

How true this seems for those who seek to follow Christ. We find within ourselves desires that draw us away from Jesus. We act in ways that are contrary to what God has said is for our highest interest. All the factors that should keep us from acting in such ways seem to be hidden when some insignificant object of desire takes center stage in our hearts.

Emotions can so easily distract us that it becomes imperative that instead of being seduced and distracted by them, we
need to attempt to train them to become allies in our quest for
a godly life. Let's say that our son was about to set out on a per-
ilous adventure that if completed could be a tremendous source
of benefit. Let's also say that we know that our son has the
resources to accomplish all it takes to complete the adventure.
But just as we know he has the resources, we also know that certain qualities of his character are going to cause problems in
this enterprise. What would we do?

I imagine that we would attempt to increase our son's understanding of how important this experience can be for the rest of
his life. We also might warn him of the consequences of starting
out on the journey but not completing it. We would want to help
him understand both of these alternatives as clearly as possible
and help him build the resolve to succeed, whatever the cost.
We would encourage him to know the dangers he will face and
also to know that the resources he brings to the task are able to
conquer the dangers. We would teach him that when he feels like
giving up, when it seems like he has nothing more to give, he
needs to focus on the finish line and the prize that awaits him
for his effort. It is this kind of focus and vision that taps into a
child's reserve of unused potential.

Now apply these same dynamics to your own spiritual life.
With all our flaws and weaknesses, we are called to an adventure
of supreme significance. All around us we are reminded of the
danger of neglecting this great task. We know these things, yet
we need more than knowledge to give our task what it requires.
We need the motivation that comes from emotional influence

to do what needs doing. We don't do what we know we should do. We don't even do what we need to do. We generally do what we are adequately motivated to do. Emotion can supply the extra impetus to move us to action.

We know that Jesus is the Son of God. Surely such knowledge alone is adequate to cause us to live holy lives. We know Jesus is the Savior of the world. Is His suffering on our behalf not enough to cause us to rid ourselves of anything that hinders our wholehearted devotion to Him? It would appear not. But if our faith has brought us to the point where we have experienced authentic affection for Jesus, and if our knowledge of His death on the cross has penetrated our minds and made its way to our hearts so that we experience genuine gratitude, then we have a whole new set of resources to motivate us to follow and obey and trust Jesus. Are not these responses to Jesus reasonable? The unreasonable response would be to have no feeling whatsoever about God's love and mercy and grace.

Some might argue that having these emotions in relationship to an invisible being makes no sense. Even Horace remarked:

Less vividly is the mind stirred by what finds entrance through
the ears than by what is bought before the trusty eyes.[3]

But the difficulty does not make the reality impossible. Even our temporal emotions do not always respond according to some fixed set of criteria. We often have more pity for the death of one individual than for the masses of humanity still slaughtered around the globe. This is not rational. Or think how the emotions respond to a story in a novel that we know to be fiction, when the scene of a battle actually taking place might not move us at all. The relationship between the emotion and the object of the emotion is almost unpredictable.

There must be some other way to stimulate our emotions in regard to Jesus and His teaching than having physical contact and proximity or having the luxury of hearing Him speak in the realm of the physical. Are sight and touch and hearing and the other instruments of contact with the physical world the only sources of generating the emotion needed to motivate our spiritual life? The answer is no! Authentic faith knows of an entirely different set of dynamics that make it possible to experience the unseen.

Jesus is not some remote abstract concept. He is a person. He is not "out there" somewhere. It is a thin veil that separates us from Him. He is present. That which obstructs our view does not change the fact that He is here. We might not see Him, but that does not stop us from knowing that He is there. Authentic faith has other ways of making contact. We can know that He is caring for us and being a father. And even though we do not see Him physically, we believe that a day is soon coming when we will. As Paul said:

> Now we see through a glass, darkly; but then face to face; now I know in part; but then shall I know even as also I am known (1 Cor. 13:12, *KJV*).

It is a different kind of knowing we experience, but it is of such a nature that all the emotion generated by physical contact in a temporal relationship can be experienced in the spiritual realm through the means of knowing Christ, who was provided by the Father. These profound feelings can help us maintain our diligence in pursuit of the spiritual life. We have a resource that is far greater than the verification of the senses. The Holy Spirit has come to live within us. It is His job to make these things experiential in our lives. The Spirit is our helper. Our inability is our great asset; it creates a humility that becomes dependent on God's grace working in us.

This spiritual principle is unknown among cultural Christians who have little understanding of the Holy Spirit or of how He works in our lives. It is virtually impossible to get to the place where you recognize your need for the Spirit and depend upon His working when you have created a safe religiosity that is perfectly manageable by means of your own abilities. The reality of empowerment by God's Spirit is experientially, if not intellectually, unknown to cultural Christians. Unwilling to take advantage of the means of authentic spirituality, they are devoid of the effects such means produce. This was not the faith of the writers of Scripture. To them, the love of Jesus was a constant reality and the power of the Spirit enabled them to live lives of authenticity in the world.

Section Three: *Faulty Thinking About the Holy Spirit*

What we have touched upon in the preceding section are the faulty ideas concerning the Holy Spirit held by the majority of professing Christians. This lack of understanding can be attributed to a large degree to the fact that cultural Christianity is not a product of biblical truth. It is the product of a religious system created by and for nominal Christians. The Bible teaches that we are powerless in and of ourselves. Jesus said, "Apart from me you can do nothing" (John 15:5). Obviously, there is much we can do apart from Jesus. But what we do apart from Him has very little to do with the realities of the kingdom of God.

A life of spiritual reality requires the enabling influence of the Holy Spirit. The risen Christ told His disciples, "You will receive power when the Holy Spirit comes on you" (Acts 1:8). It is the job of the Holy Spirit to enlighten our understanding, purify our minds, and work in our lives to help us become conformed to the image of Christ. The Holy Spirit creates authentic faith. He works in our lives to help us understand our need: He brings us to a point of conviction of our sin: He helps us understand who Jesus is and what He has done. Some would even say He gives us the ability to turn to Christ and repent. He responds to our repentance by enabling us to believe, and having made belief possible, He enters the human personality with His presence in order that Christ might dwell in us. The Holy Spirit brings all that the Father decreed, and all that the Son accomplished, into our experience. It is impossible to have authentic faith apart from the operations of the Spirit. As Paul said, "If anyone does not have the Spirit of Christ, he does not belong to Christ" (Rom. 8:9).

The Bible is so clear on these things that you would think it would be impossible to call oneself a Christian and yet deny these truths. History and experience demonstrate that this is true spirituality. The Liturgy of the Church affirms it.

Section Four: *Faulty Thinking About Acceptance with God*

So what have we found? First, many cultural Christians have little understanding of what the Bible teaches about the workings of the Holy Spirit, this wonderful gift that comes because of what Christ has done and is the first hint that something has really happened in our lives. Second, many of the same men and women hold such lukewarm feelings toward Jesus because of their lack of understanding of what the Bible teaches about the true state of their souls. What is the source of this faulty thinking?

If we take a close look at the very foundations of thought that have led to these misconceptions, I believe we will find that the root problem lies with faulty thinking about what is required for us to live in a relationship of acceptance with God. We will often find that the nominal Christian (using the term in its more cultural sense) holds very superficial and dangerous notions about this subject. It seems incomprehensible, when we consider the enormous price Christ paid for our sin, that some can still think that some general principle of mercy or, even worse, that some weighing of our good deeds against our bad is adequate grounds for fallen humanity to stand in right relationship with God.

Is it enough to consider oneself a good person if one has done no crime against society? Or to think that even though one might violate God's commands, one does it infrequently and is usually being tricked into it? When someone thinks like this, it is inevitable that a self-evaluation of good deeds and bad deeds will come out on the positive side of the ledger. Such a person doesn't deny the existence of Jesus. He or she actually often uses His name in prayer and attempts to demonstrate some measure of conformity to what he or she believes to be Christian behavior. But that person doesn't seem to understand the meaning of what redemption in Christ actually entails.

Others go a bit further in their thinking. They have some sense that it is what Christ has done that makes us acceptable to God. But their ideas don't involve any personal commitment or responsibility. It is as if the death of Jesus changed the nature of the moral universe and now God can be more liberal in His treatment of sin. They think that if they don't sin too much and live a reasonably good life, they will get to heaven.

I know there is a danger in speaking of what goes on in the heart of another person. I know also that the subtleties of language can create misunderstanding. But for those who understand the biblical teaching on these subjects, it is not difficult to identify that often the people who use even some of the right language are not really relying on the redemptive work of Christ or God's grace as much as on their own efforts to achieve their own ideas of what it takes to live in a proper relationship with God. Their focus is on their own accomplishments, not on Jesus Christ and His sacrifice.

When we think like this, it is almost impossible to come to grips with the inadequacy of our own efforts or the impossibility of fully meeting the obligations of God's Word. We create an illusion that will keep us from acknowledging our own guilt and helplessness. We have not come to terms with our inability before God. ALL THIS FAULTY THINKING IS THE RESULT OF HOLDING MISTAKEN CONCEPTIONS OF THE BASIC PRINCIPLES OF CHRISTIANITY.[4]

Authentic Christianity is a way for the most wayward of men and women to enter into a right relationship with God based solely on the fact that "while we were yet sinners, Christ died for us" (Rom. 5:8, *KJV*). They have confused the outcome of getting right with God with the means of getting right with Him. Only when we have come empty-handed to the foot of the cross and cried out for God's mercy and grace, and been reborn by the indwelling of the Holy Spirit, can we even begin to live the life to which God calls us. Some seem to think that Christ has made it possible for them to be right with God because His death has somehow lowered God's standards to the level of their perform-ance. In their confusion, they will even tell others that this is the message of the gospel.

The results of this foundational error are predictable. Those who operate under this system will fail to come to grips with their own true state. They will have little sense of gratitude for all that Christ has done and continues to do so that they might be reconciled to God. They have struck a deal with God: "I'll do my part and You accept me." When encountering those whom they deem less worthy of God's love than they are, their message is one of reformation of behavior in order to become a Christian. They will not be able to rightly communicate the bib-lical message that what is required is an absolute abandonment to what Christ has done on their behalf to provide forgiveness and life.

I am hopeful that if I keep repeating myself on this matter, it will be impossible for you to misunderstand my meaning. This is a matter of the heart. God sees your heart and knows when you trust Him to forgive you. By now I hope you see how the faulty thinking of our time has led to both the lack of affection for Jesus and the disregard concerning the work of the Holy Spirit that so characterizes cultural Christianity in our nation today. It seems to be a natural explanation for the state of things. If we are to experience the vitality that the apostolic church enjoyed, we must, like the apostle Paul, have the attitude, "May I never boast except in the cross of our Lord Jesus Christ" (Gal. 6:14).

I hope you will not mistake what I am saying here. I'm sure that on the day we stand in the presence of Christ, we will discover that there are some who understand these things and affirm them but whose lives show no evidence that Christ has transformed them. Authentic faith will always be evidenced by changed lives. Surely this is what Christ meant when He referred to those who take His name and yet on the last day will hear the dreadful words: "I never knew you. Away from me, you evildoers!" (Matt. 7:23).

When all these truths coalesce, we see what is required of us: a total dependence on the atonement of Christ and the empowerment to live a life that pleases Him made possible by the workings of the Holy Spirit in our lives; a surrender to Christ, not only as Savior, but also as Lord of our lives; a resolve to learn from the Bible and to live a life of obedience to Christ's commandments.

I hope I am not making this too complicated. I did start out to write these things in a way that was intended for all to understand. It comes down to this: What is the true state of your heart? For the simple of heart, trusting totally on Christ for all this is not a problem. For those whose hearts have been obscured by their pride and intellect, such things might seem foolish.

Of course, that is exactly what Paul said. The wisdom of God is thought to be foolishness by the vain wisdom of man. The simple-hearted are less likely to be hindered in understanding these things by the seductions of ambition and worldly grandeur. They are not as likely to be led astray by the cares and pleasures of life. They are more able to respond to Christ with humility, penitence and sincerity. They might not be able to launch into a lofty discourse about the nature of emotions, but they can feel love for their families, friends and country.

There are those who also hold that even though the death of Christ and the workings of the Holy Spirit are to be affirmed as basic articles of our faith, they are so beyond our comprehension that we should turn our attention to those things we can better understand. By this they refer to the practical and moral precepts of the gospel. Their argument would suggest that it is these practical matters that we can know and on which we should thus focus our attention. They reduce the gospel to a system of morality and discount the importance of the mysteries of the Bible. They have bought into what Milton called:

Vain Wisdom all, and false philosophy![5]

For those who attempt to reduce faith to a system of ethics, we respond with the words of Jesus: "The work of God is this: to believe in the one he has sent" (John 6:29). The arguments against authentic faith are so complicated and yet flimsy at the same time, one wonders how anyone can actually hold such positions. Some may say that we should not spend our time focusing on the more heavenly things that have no application to real life.

That certainly was not the thinking of the apostles in the New Testament. These men continually exhorted their audience to attend to the doctrines of the faith. Read the Epistles. Notice how often particular doctrines of the faith are mentioned and made the center of the writer's attention. Also notice the pattern that the practical matters of ethics and behavior are often connected to these doctrines as the expected outcome of faith. When you see the predominance of this pattern in the letters, you have to come to the conclusion that the Christianity practiced by many is an *unscriptural* religion.[6]

Let us apply these things to our own lives. Have we cast ourselves completely on the grace of God and the work of Christ? Do we consider these the only source of hope in life? Are we progressing in our affection for the Lord and taking advantage of all resources provided by Him to deepen our love? I think we should bow humbly before the throne of God in prayer and seek the pardon and grace given to us by Jesus. I think we should ask God to create in us a spirit of true repentance and undivided faith in Jesus Christ. I think we should continually strive in these things so that we are not satisfied until we love Him fully. I think we should pray that we would be filled with joy and peace and hope through the work of the Holy Spirit in our lives. I think we should diligently study the Bible so that our affection is rooted and rational. As we meditate on the passion of the Lord and as we worship Him in prayer and praise, we should attempt to practice the presence of Jesus continually.

It makes no sense to take the name of Christian and not cling to Christ. Jesus is not some magic charm to wear like a piece of jewelry we think will give us good luck. He is the Lord.

His name is to be written on our hearts in such a powerful way that it creates within us a profound experience of His peace and a heart that is filled with His praise.

Notes
1. Tacitus, *Agricola*, bk. 30.
2. Ovid, *Metamorphoses*, bk. 7, lines 20-21.
3. Horace, *Ars Poetica*, lines 180-181.
4. Wilberforce puts this sentence in capital letters.
5. John Milton, *Paradise Lost*, bk. 2, line 565.
6. Wilberforce italicizes the word "unscriptural."

TRUE STANDARDS OF CHRISTIAN BEHAVIOR

Section One: *How Belief Influences Behavior* [1]

You may wonder about the title of this chapter in light of what has preceded. One might think that if an inadequate understanding of Jesus and the work of the Cross had led someone to a faith that thinks acceptance with God is based on performance, a kind of religious experience of the greatest strictness would be generated.

What we see is the opposite. Those who hold to the biblical doctrines of the work of Christ as the basis of acceptance tend also to take the Bible's instructions concerning righteous living more seriously. Those who have created a system of their own tend to water down what is required in the practice of their faith. They also tend to create standards of behavior that fit their own lifestyles; standards that they know they can meet without the need of supernatural assistance. The outcome is a way of life that is characterized by ignorance and conceit.

It seems that in our day it is the commonly held belief that if a man or woman says he or she is a Christian, even when not knowing what that really means, and if he or she is not guilty of some gross violation of the accepted cultural morality, no one questions whether or not that person is indeed a Christian. The word "Christian" implies no more than a sort of general assent to Christianity and a degree of morality in life that is little different from the good Hindu, Muslim or Buddhist.

If you doubt that this is the state of much of the Christian world, ask yourself whether most cultural Christians would experience much of a change in either their behavior or thinking if it were irrefutably proven that Christianity was not true. Would they still attend church as a social responsibility? Would the knowledge that the Bible is not true change the way they sought counsel, modeled their behavior or sought a sense of meaning and purpose?

Of course, these are unnecessary questions. We already have examples of the lives of unbelievers that are morally superior to many who say they are Christians. We have the most superior moral system in existence. Yet if we don't live by it, what good is it?

We say that Jesus is our Savior, but we forget that He also said He was our example. He not only said, "Believe in me," but also, "Follow me!" It certainly is not the case that the early followers of Jesus lived less moral lives than the lives of those around them. They lived as Jesus lived, and the world took notice.

Someone might argue that the morality of Christianity has so raised the standard that even unbelievers have recognized it as a goal to strive toward. They might praise the morality of Christianity while denying the doctrines it teaches. Is this possible? Are the foundations of faith of so little significance to the practice of faith that they are irrelevant to practical living? If so, it is tragic that the cost paid to establish those doctrines was so high. Did Christ die in vain? If so, how can we say that those who believe have been given eternal life while those who reject Christ are objects of the wrath of God? That would certainly be unfair. Yet what we see today in Christendom is a practice of Christian faith that often produces no greater morality than that practiced by those who categorically deny the essentials of the Christian faith. Something is obviously wrong here. It is my conviction that the problem lies with a faulty understanding of what God requires of us in terms of practical Christian living.

The Bible teaches that we are to be holy and even perfect as God Himself is perfect. These commands are almost universally dismissed as a type of hyperbole, not really intended to impact our behavior. Yet a careful study of the Bible reveals that these are not isolated instructions. The plain teaching of the apostles demanded a strict standard of Christian morality and behavior. Christian character is to be a reflection of living in relationship with a holy God.

This character is first and foremost a product of understanding and embracing the finished work of Christ on our behalf and of unreservedly devoting ourselves to God. This is the very image represented in baptism: We die to the old way of living and rise to a new way of life. We might think about using the analogy of Hannibal's father committing the infant Hannibal to become an eternal champion, waging war against all the enemies of Carthage. In the same way, God has called us to be the sworn enemies of sin. We are to wage war against it and strive to give it no opportunity in our lives.

Having made a commitment to Christ, we are to yield ourselves without reserve to the service of our King. We are no longer our own. All that we are belongs to Christ. We are to become instruments set apart for the honor and glory of God. This is the ruling principle that is to guide all we do. Whatever has been the motivating force of our lives before Christ is either to be abandoned or to take a distant second to this. We are to be submitted to the Lordship of Christ. The motto of authentic faith is this: "Do it all for the glory of God" (1 Cor. 10:31).

When these convictions guide us, we will have the seeds of all true virtue sown within our hearts. The seed will germinate and the roots begin to grow deep into our inner life. As we progress in our faith, the seed will ultimately break through and bear abundant fruit. This is the source of Christian morality. As Virgil wrote:

Fiery is the vigor and divine the source of those life-seeds.[2]

Ultimately, this is the character that will thrive forever in the eternal presence of God. For the present, however, living this way has challenges. Not only is Christ in us, but also our old fallen nature is still in us. The Holy Spirit has supernaturally imparted the nature of Christ to us. Our fallen nature has been with us from birth. These two will not live together in harmony. We will experience constant reminders of the conflict of the two, yet we will have a fixed desire and determination to pursue conformity to the character of Christ. It is this resolution that distinguishes authentic faith from cultural Christianity.

I should make it clear that this is not a task filled with drudgery. When a man or woman possesses authentic faith, the pursuit of holiness is a joy. Such individuals have the sense that because God is all knowing and all loving, His will for their lives is the one that will produce the greatest benefit for them. When you put the pieces together, you see that authentic faith is motivated toward obedience to the will of God by an understanding of the glory of God, by a sense of trust and hope in Him, with an appreciation and awe for His goodness, in a spirit of joyfulness, and with continual gratitude.

In case you are reading this and are discouraged about how far you have to go, let me encourage you. The dynamics I have laid out here may exist in various degrees and proportions. Differences in personality, life circumstances, spiritual maturity and other factors will all influence character development. There may be different degrees of love, or reverence, or trust in different Christians. In one, love might be the dominant motivator. In another, it might be reverence. The key is that in greater or lesser degrees, authentic faith will be characterized by some measure of all these factors. The common denominator among those possessing authentic faith is the determination to devote themselves to the service and glory of God. The other common characteristic is an awareness of how inadequate they are to achieve this goal without grace and empowerment.

To those who might argue that this measure of devotion is one reserved for some special class of Christians, it must be pointed out that the Bible itself makes no such distinction. The instructions concerning what is expected of the believer are stated in such general terms that we must draw the conclusion that they are intended for all Christians. No one is exempt. The Bible is filled with ample evidence that the teachings of Christ and the apostles are universal in their application. They apply to *all*

Christians. Since the motivating principles for a life of joyful obedience are the same for all, it is only logical that the response to
these factors would be universal as well. All Christians are to be *servants* and *children* of God (see Matt. 5:45; John 3:5; Rom. 8:9,14-
15; 1 Cor. 6:19-20).[3] All are to serve Him and submit to Him with
the attitudes and actions that belong to such relationships.

Jesus said that the greatest commandment was "Love the
Lord your God with all your heart and with all your soul and
with all your mind and with all your strength" (Mark 12:30).
If these words have any meaning at all, they validate all that has
been said. The love of God is the basic requirement for authentic faith. It is not reserved or demanded for a chosen few. God is
not looking for a divided heart. Heavenly treasure is to be our
primary pursuit. Even love of family is to be secondary to our
love of Christ. A lukewarm faith is an affront to all we affirm
about Him.

God is not interested in sharing His glory with any com-
petitor. The Bible is filled with this truth. To place the glory of
anything over the glory of God is idolatry. When the supreme
love of the heart is directed toward anything other than God,
idolatry has taken place. Whatever draws our heart from Him,
engrosses our minds or holds the number one spot in our affections is an idol. Only God is to be the object of our supreme
worship.

As clear as the Bible is on this subject, it seems baffling at
how frequently it is disregarded. These are things we must take
seriously. If we do, our attitude will not be one of complacency.
On the contrary, these things will be our passion. Unreserved
commitment to the glory and service of God is the foundation

on which all Christian behavior will be built. Once firmly in place, it will serve to help us be and do all God desires.

Section Two: *The Behavior of the Cultural Christian*[4]

Having established the parameters and character of true faith, let us investigate in a little more detail the cultural Christianity that exists all around us.

I formerly made the observation that faith has become a subject that is held at arm's length these days. Now I want to look at those who come a little closer to true belief but not close enough to know with some measure of mastery the intricacies of Christian faith. I don't presume to suggest that the various ideas I talk about are found with great precision in every person who embodies a cultural faith rather than a biblical one. I do believe that I will be able to point out general themes and outlines that characterize this group of men and women. I can tell you what a face is and what it generally looks like, but in no way does that describe the uniqueness of every face. That would be impossible.

At the risk of repeating myself, let me point out the false thinking that exists about the nature of authentic faith. True faith is something that so pervades our lives that it affects everything we do. It is a matter of the heart, where its reality becomes our supreme influence. It seeks to root out anything that is contrary to its truth and attempts to bring all the heart's desires and affections under its control.

We believe that when we come to faith, Christ comes to dwell in our lives by the presence of the Holy Spirit. This is a foundation of true faith that forces us to measure all we do against this reality.

Any thought or action that is inconsistent with this truth is defective and to be resisted. The Holy Spirit becomes our ultimate motivation. His presence permeates and penetrates every fiber of our being.

But the thinking of many among us is an altogether different beast. Such thinking begins by creating a set of standards that acknowledges some actions must be stopped, and then a conceptual framework is created that regulates this set of standards. But this framework exists within a larger context, or paradigm. Faith only operates within the smaller framework, while life is lived in the larger context. Only certain thoughts, time, resources and influences are under the jurisdiction of faith. The individual remains master of the rest that falls outside this self-constructed box. *Faith is for Sunday,* such an individual thinks. *If I meet my religious obligations, I am free to live my life as I wish.* Thus the reality and work of the Spirit are held captive in a diminished role in their lives. Authentic faith is not allowed to expand and possess more of the individual's life. Its influence is limited and ineffective.

When Christ is not free to possess more and more of who we are, the tendency over time is to take even what we have placed within the smaller framework and move it out into the larger context. We will actually regress spiritually instead of progressing in authentic spirituality. By nature, the outer realities and its values will press hard against the seeming restrictions of true faith. The space occupied by faith will diminish over time, until it is hardly active at all. We will become a nominal possessor of that which we profess. This is the genesis of cultural Christianity.

I fear that this is more the rule than the exception among us. The general state of Christianity is much more cultural than authentic. The advancement of the kingdom of God and His glory are scarcely embraced as the objects of our greatest passions. The pursuit of these treasures is no longer what we strive for. Christ is not Lord over all our lives. We have made ourselves our own masters. Life gets confusing. What was to be our highest pursuit is lost as our minds and hearts become consumed with lesser issues. If our thinking and our power are our own, then possessions become property rather than objects of stewardship. At best, we give our leftovers to God and keep the rest, indulging ourselves in the full and free pursuit of personal pleasure.

This is the reason why we see so little sense of spiritual responsibility attached to high position, incredible ability or great fortunes. Christ's instructions concerning faithful stewardship of all we are and all we have are forgotten. If there is any sense of obligation, it is usually referenced as our duty to the good of society or the welfare of our families, and even these references are only regulated by our own comfort and self-interest. Personal pleasure and personal peace become the regulators of where we live, where we work, how we spend our time, what we think, what we say and how we amuse ourselves. The great issue of our lives becomes boredom. What a tragedy!

To live our lives and miss that great purpose we were designed to accomplish is truly a sin. It is inconceivable that we could be bored in a world with so much wrong to tackle, so much ignorance to teach and so much misery we could alleviate. It seems that ambition and avarice know no boundaries.

Yet life goes on with too many living in a kind of shapeless idleness. Recreation becomes the goal of life. Pubs abound, sports are perpetually proliferating, gambling consumes many, and almost any form of entertainment is pursued to fill the void created by a meaningless life. Year after year goes by in unprofitable pursuit. Young and old alike live for things that do not satisfy and ignore the very things that bring fulfillment. We are not criminals or murderers or thieves. Our sin is not so obvious. We live according to the standards of society, drifting along on this world's ideas of living, oblivious to the consequences.

To fill the void of meaninglessness, some turn to sensual pleasures. I'm not speaking here of those who are blatantly immoral and reject the Christian faith. I am referring to those who put on a front of morality and virtue and even call themselves Christians. Outwardly, all looks well, but in their private lives they are as immoral as the blatant pagan. They are closet sensualists. The Bible instructs us to put to death the deeds of the sin nature, but through habitual indulgence, the way of the old nature has become the norm for the majority of modern Christians. The idea of exercising vigilant restraint and self-denial is viewed as something belonging to the residents of monasteries.

Authentic Christian discipleship requires a kind of diligent watchfulness. Those of whom we speak have forgotten their responsibility to serve God and their fellowman. They act as if the norm for a Christian was a life of constant indulgence. To live in more affluence, with more sensual pleasure and luxury, is the chief aim of their lives. Even the healthy practice of staying in shape has become an end in and of itself instead of a means to be more effective as a servant. Health and exercise become such an obsession that they constitute another form of sensual indulgence.

Others find different ways to express this attitude. They pursue possessions, prestige, power and position, as if these things make life meaningful. Numerous cultural Christians have their hearts set on the acquisition of these things as the primary purpose of their lives. It is ironic, however, that those who actually possess these things are much less affected by them than those who pursue what they do not have. Those who do not have them are held captive by pretense and the appearance of things rather than the actual reality. What a contrast to the humble and modest lifestyle Jesus taught and demonstrated. Instead of humility, vanity is the predominant disposition of the hearts of these cultural Christians.

The problem of sensuality is only one area in which cultural Christians fail to pursue the purposes of God. Money and ambition have become idols in our time, especially for individuals in the business and professional worlds. Disguised as common business practice, these forces are allowed to gather great momentum in our lives. Arguments about being diligent at what we do, becoming successful in our profession or providing for our families seduce us so that we no longer have a clear sense of judgment about these issues. Our work consumes us. The fatigue produced by it causes us to seek out worldly leisure to provide refreshment of our souls at the expense of the means of spiritual refreshing. We work, we play, we work, and we play—but our spirits are neglected in the cycle.

When God begins to stir our souls with the anxiety that something is not right, we respond by seeking distraction. We look to social gatherings or amusements to smother the rising anxiety.

The great distraction for the businessperson is to lose himself or herself in work, declaring that there's no time to think about spiritual matters. These people are always looking for that coming season when they will have enough time to pay attention to the matters that matter most. Business and pleasure fill their time, and the spiritual life gets neglected.

I won't take more of your time by demonstrating that the politician, the philosopher, the scholar, the poet, the artist and others have their own variation of this routine. It is enough to point out that each has his or her own pursuits that become the primary obsession. All act as if their happiness is totally dependent on the success or failure of their work. Don't misunderstand what I am saying. Culture, art, education and business all have their place. The problem occurs when the place that faith is to play in our lives is preempted by these lesser pursuits. Their value is exactly proportionate to the importance of temporal existence measured against eternity.

Often, it is not possible to identify any one supreme passion that has distracted us from the pursuit of God. The various threads of our lives are so intermingled and diversified that we are not always able to identify where our distraction lies. We no longer have the ability to follow the advice of Socrates to "know thyself!" Further, we have failed to listen to the wisdom of Solomon to "above all else, guard your heart" (Prov. 4:23). Most men and women are ignorant of their true state and oblivious to the things that have replaced God in their lives.

But if it is true that the Bible teaches that the supreme object of our affections is to be God and if in fact any of these things that distract us have taken the place only He rightfully deserves, then in truth we have become disloyal to God. God desires to set up His throne in our hearts and reign there without a rival. In some, the revolt is obvious and overt. In others, it is hidden. But in both cases, we have become estranged from our rightful Lord. Giving our supreme devotion to a career is just as much an act of spiritual treason as giving our body to acts of immorality or our energies to greed and thievery. The external appearances might be different, but the principal is the same. If we do not return our allegiance to its rightful Lord, we will suffer the consequences when the things that are highly valued by men are shown to be nothing but abominations in the eyes of God.

This way of thinking has become rare in our time. Most men and women no longer view life through a spiritual grid. Even when we recognize that certain individuals are lazy and thoughtless, wasting their life in meaningless and trivial ways, we evaluate them in terms of temporal values and not in terms of the consequences of their lifestyles in relationship to the eternal. Excessive vanity and uncontrolled ambition are viewed as character flaws, not sins. If a friend is sick or suffering physically, we are concerned to the extent that we will attempt to prescribe some remedy that might alleviate his or her ailment. But when a friend is spiritually ill, we do very little to help alleviate this illness. We avoid confrontation, hoping that some third party might come along and minister to him or her.

We treat our own children as though they are only temporal creatures. When we must help them determine where they will get their education, what they will study, who they will marry or what career they will choose, we often fail to process these decisions through the filter of God's eternal kingdom. We look at how these decisions will affect their potential economically or in terms of cultural norms of success, but rarely do we take into account eternal issues. Careful examination of what we do in these cases reveals what is of most importance in our thinking.

These are the logical consequences of making the error we have looked at before: not considering authentic faith of enough value to make it the motivating principle of our lives. Robbed of its rightful place, faith and religion turn into a cold and lifeless system of rules and regulations. We look at God's laws as restrictive and punitive. We treat them is if they are restrictions on our freedom. We resent even the restrictions placed on actions we don't even desire to take. As the Greek poet Juvenal says:

Even those who don't want to kill anybody would like to have the power to do it.[5]

Even when we give attention to these decrees, we tend to interpret them in ways that favor our lifestyles. Sometimes we do this by fulfilling the letter of the law without giving any consideration to the spirit of the law that is behind the letter. If we knew the Bible better, we would be more concerned with the spirit than with the letter. We attempt to skirt the Bible's teachings by rationalizing that the culture of that time was much different from our own. We say that the culture of that time required stricter prohibitions because of its limitations. We try to explain truth away as being only figurative or hyperbolic. Surely, God would not have us keep these instructions strictly and literally!

Using linguistic gymnastics or other rationalizations (which we never really believe), we systematically explain away the moral requirements of the Word of God. If all attempts to explain them away have failed, we then simply decide that we ought to give ourselves some grace in these things.

When even this fails to rid of us of these pesky requirements, we break them, hoping that our sin is not all that problematic: a little harmless joking, a few foolish expletives, a bit of colorful humor. We argue, "Even deeply religious men indulge periodically in such actions, don't they?" We even use the mercy of God as an excuse to indulge ourselves. "Surely God wouldn't judge that!" We appeal our case to the universal understanding of the weakness of humanity. In the words of the Latin proverb, "The law does not regard trifles." All men are weak. We confess it, wish we were better and trust that as we age we will become so. With a false sense of humility, we declare that only the grace of God will help us spend eternity with Him.

Don't misunderstand me. It is absolutely true that only the grace of God gives us hope. But this is not said with true humility. True humility feels the burden of these truths and longs to be free from the burden of sin. Sin becomes hideous to us. We long not to grieve God. But those who use these great truths as rationalizations have no such attitude. Their lives reveal that they enjoy living on the edge of sin. They like to play with fire. They have no love for holiness and no desire to acquire it.

It is a lamentable consequence of thinking of religion as a set of rules, rather than as an internal principle, that it soon becomes to us an external system of behavior rather that a habit of the mind and heart. This will only work for so long. Eventually, even the individual who appears to have mastered the external issues without actually having internalized the spirit will find his or her approach to faith as effective as the architect who decides not to waste his time building a foundation before he begins to erect the superstructure. We all know the fate of such a building!

There is a fascinating dynamic in all of this. We all know that our faith in Christ is not merely a matter of internal belief. If our conduct does not conform to that belief, then our belief can be called into question. The latter validates the former. It is almost impossible to live as Christ taught if we do not have a transforming belief that changes the way we live. So the latter depends on the former as well as the former needing the accompaniment of the latter.

Jesus said we will know a tree by its fruit, but He also indicated that it is necessary to make the tree good in order for it to bear good fruit (see Matt. 7:17-20). The Bible continuously instructs us to pay careful attention to our hearts, or inner being. The true state of the heart is of ultimate importance to God. If the heart is good, the external behavior will reflect this. External actions are reflections of the state of the heart. Jesus said, "For out of the overflow of the heart the mouth speaks" (Matt. 12:34). This is a primary difference between the cultural Christianity of our day and authentic faith. Cultural Christianity is primarily concerned with externals. It does not understand how the internal realities of authentic faith are what make the externals possible in the way Jesus desires.

Although this may seem obvious to many, the principle of judging faith on the basis of internal principles is diametrically opposed to judging it on the basis of external actions. When we recognize the importance of the internal dimensions of faith, we will become vigilant in keeping our hearts right before God. If our focus is on external actions alone, the very state of the heart tends to deteriorate like the seed planted among the thorns. The thorns of human nature grow unattended and eventually choke out the good seed. The garden of the heart must be tended with great care. What we see in the current state of Christianity is a near total disregard for any effort to cultivate the heart. When the state of the heart and mind is not cared for, the door is opened for the unobstructed growth of thoughts and attitudes that lead to spiritual catastrophe. It is not until the external becomes obvious that we realize what has happened.

Because of this dynamic, God instructs us to "live by faith" (2 Cor. 5:7). Usually, this phrase is used to encourage us when we can't see the reason for the difficult circumstances that are making our lives hard. We are told that we need to believe, even in the midst of such difficulty. This is certainly part of what the phrase means. But in a more universal sense, it is an exhortation to continually allow our faith—our relationship with Christ—to be the habitual dynamic by which we live out our days. We must walk (live) by faith as the motivating and ruling dynamic of our life. When we live this way, it creates a new kind of vision for our life.

Think of "vision" here as representing a life based on our perception of the world as we experience it in our fallen state. When we live according to the faith dynamic, we see life from a different perspective. We see it through the lens of God's truth. The unseen becomes seen. Such a way of operating takes mental and spiritual vigilance. It is generally unknown, and certainly misunderstood, by the majority of cultural Christians who are merely attempting to be good. This does not mean that we attempt to escape the material world and live in some spiritual unreality. Rather, keeping the mind attuned to the truth of God, we live active and productive lives and enjoy the comforts and blessings of the material world with a proper sense of moderation and thankfulness. We are careful not to live *totus in illis* ("totally absorbed in those matters").

Authentic faith works to keep the eternal in focus. This kind of attitude contrasts sharply with that of nominal Christians who are almost entirely preoccupied with the concerns of this world. Even though they know in their minds that life is fleeting, this information does not penetrate their hearts. Contrast these individuals with the Christians who keep a steady focus on the things that are really important to God. They have a sense of perspective that enables them to handle the uncertainties of life with a sense of dignified composure. They are comfortable enough with themselves to be able to reach out to serve others.

But this is not all. One other significant difference between nominal Christians and real Christians is the spirit in which they act in relationship to even the external things. Nominal Christians often do the correct external action, but rarely without some sense of deprivation or duty. Authentic believers recognize how the external demands of Christianity are expressions of the love of God. They are able to live obediently with a sense of willing, even joyful, action. That is not to say they do not need support and encouragement or that they don't need to keep their thinking renewed. They know that without such vigilance, they are prone to having the former objects of their desire resume their influence. They keep guard over their hearts and minds and work at increasing their knowledge and love of heavenly things.

The Bible is filled with confirmation that this is the way to live an authentic spiritual life. The believer is told that having his or her affections set on things above is not in vain. It would seem that to the cultural Christian, faith and pleasure are contradictory. This is not the picture we get in the Bible. On the contrary, it speaks of the way of Christ as the path of peace and joy. The one who is steadfast in the pursuit of God is pictured as the person who has a calm and grateful spirit that reflects the fact that this is a person who is in harmony with himself or herself and all that is around him or her.

Another example of the difference between these two kinds of faith is what we see in reference to Sundays. This is a day that God Himself set aside to be a special day. It was designed to be a day when spiritual issues could be especially focused upon. We are told that on this day, we should lay aside the business and cares of life to spend time with God. The intention was that this would be a joyful day of fellowship. But is it? How do cultural Christians spend this day? Do they enter God's gates with gladness? After church, if they go, how do they spend the rest of this day? Do they spend the day cultivating their relationship with God? Do they reach out to others to help them with their growth in Christ? Do they use their time seeking to serve the kingdom of God?

You would think that setting aside one day for these purposes would not seem problematic. Properly understood, it should be viewed as a great blessing. Unfortunately, this is not the case. Instead of experiencing the day as a day of spiritual opportunity, a day of reflection and adjustment, a day to correct the errors that might have accumulated during the week, or a day of joy, love and harmony, many abuse the day through the sense of obligation they attach to it or by totally disregarding it. It seems to them a chore to devote a whole day to God. If they attend church at all, they deem it a merit entitling them to spend the rest of the day as they please. They find it much easier to utilize Sunday to finish work started during the week than to take the exercises of Sunday and insert them into the middle of the week. They find all kinds of excuses to do tasks that are really not that important to accomplish at all. For many, business itself is viewed as more recreational than enduring what they feel to be the drudgery of Sunday!

There are those who find themselves having the right attitude to the devotional life and especially the role Sunday plays in it. They are concerned about this state and pray with humility that they might be more effective in keeping times of devotion and worship. They desire a heart that is more hungry for spiritual things and less consumed by the enjoyments of the temporal world. If you are one of these people, do not be discouraged. I am not speaking about you. I am speaking of those who know this to be their condition and yet have no concern about it. They live their lives as if they had no thought for God at all.

This is not the only area in which nominal Christians have a problem. They justify their own deficiencies by asserting that those who strive to please God in this area of behavior are seeking a higher type of faith than that to which they aspire. Their own lives lack the qualities of kindness, gentleness, patience and, above all, the humility that more than any other virtue is the essence and critical component of true Christian character. Not only are these virtues not sought, but the very opposite is turned into a kind of virtue by talk of a "just" pride or a "proper" pride. These kinds of expressions have been invented to justify a warped vanity and self-centeredness. This is such an important subject that it merits a separate section to explore.

Section Three: *The Concern About What People Think About Us Compared to the Attitude of Authentic Christianity*

The desire to be admired by other people, in all its various forms, has come to totally consume most people in our culture. Even though we often think this problem belongs only to the upper classes, the fact is that it dominates both sexes and all social classes. It takes many forms and hides itself in many disguises. It permeates all we think, speak and do. Sometimes it is openly acknowledged, but even when it is not, it is often the underlying motivation that guides many men and women and is often the master passion of the soul.

This is a way of thinking that begins in the cradle and is reinforced throughout a lifetime. It is often the expressed goal of schools and colleges to cultivate this attitude under the guise of achievement and success. Some would even go so far as to say that without this principle at work, we would destroy our civilization and its comforts as we now know them. They then qualify their statements by affirming that we should not abandon our values or duty in order to attain the favor of men, or in fear of the disapproval of men. But in practice, this qualification is rarely observed.

Sometimes, the love of praise is blatantly ridiculous. Sometimes it is sinister. It is responsible at times for heroes and at other times for villains. Those who advocate the virtue of the principle might say that all of what I have spoken so far is a perversion of the true principle and that when used with the proper motivation, it has powerful positive outcomes. They might argue that it is this principle, properly motivated, that leads to the pursuit of excellence in virtuous enterprises, the development of skills that can be used for positive purposes, a kind of courage that cannot be deterred and a perseverance that enables us to finish the race.

They might also argue that when the motivation is proper, this principle can keep a rich man from wasting his life in sensual pleasures and motivate him to a life of productivity. They would go on to point out how it might motivate a man or woman to pursue toil and endure hardship instead of wasting life enjoying the pleasures of someone else's labors. They point out how it can be a force that keeps the privileged from misusing their privilege and give the underprivileged the motivation to seek to overcome their difficult circumstances.

It is further suggested that it is not all bad to want to please. It can lead to courtesy and good will. It can create a positive environment in interpersonal relationships. Even in our private moments, we often do the right thing as if watched by an imaginary spectator. It is argued that we should not reject such a tool that helps us act properly when virtue alone doesn't motivate us.

All these arguments sound good. The problem is that they don't work. This kind of approach to life shifts with the changes of the prevailing culture. What is acceptable in one generation is not in the next. What is abhorred in one is embraced in another. It is a principle that under the right circumstances supports vice and resists justice. It produces the appearance of virtue, but not the reality. Even the philosophers and poets of the ancient world saw through its falseness.

There is only one way this principle legitimately operates. This is when our desire to please is not directed at other men and women, but at God. To please God is a wonderful motivator toward that which is good and lovely. The desire to please man is full of dangers. The Bible has much to say about the subject.

The biblical view of this principle is quite different from that held by many professing Christians. Rather than this desire being held in high esteem, the Bible teaches that the state of mind most conducive to our true condition is one of humility and recognition of the extent of our flaws. We are told that in order to live in a way that pleases God, we need to aggressively fight against our natural tendencies toward arrogance and self-importance. Any natural advantages we might have over another, or any progress in virtue, should be viewed as the work of God in our lives. We could say that the primary purpose of much of the Bible in general and the Gospels in particular is to teach us to reject pride and selfishness and their consequences; to enable us to understand our defects and problems in a way that creates a sense of humility; and because of the work of Christ applied in our lives, to live to the glory of God, not self. God alone is to be exalted. All our glory is to be turned to the glory of God.

It seems that these instructions are generally rejected. Those who write about morality often totally ignore the internal motivation of an action. If the desire to gain the applause of men leads to action that is beneficial to society, it is viewed as a good thing. But the Bible teaches that this desire for human admiration is in itself a problem. It leads to a corrupt motivation that in the end seeks to give credit and glory to man instead of attributing all good things to the One to whom the glory belongs. Whether the outcome of this motivation is good or bad, it still glorifies humanity, not God.

If we take the Bible's evaluation of the nature of man as accurate, we need to understand that the world's commendations or condemnations may be skewed and twisted. Such praise or criticism comes from a way of thinking that the Bible says is darkened and depraved. Even giving praise to such actions that are set forth in Scripture, which lead to a better standard of living, can be a problem. Eventually, the lack of proper focus in giving accolades can even lead to promoting certain behavior as admirable when it in no way reflects what God has asked of us. For this reason, it is important that authentic faith distrusts any praise lavished on a person, particularly when it is excessive. Rather than allowing it to puff up the recipient, it should be used as a warning against human vanity.

One of the problems of receiving such praise is the effect it has on keeping our focus on eternal things. The Bible tells us that we are to set our minds on the things that are "above" and "eternal." But human praise tends to distract us with earthly concerns. It also seems to lend itself to self-reinforcement so that when we receive the applause of men, we want more of it. Suddenly, we discover that the good opinions of others and the praise of men have gained a foothold in our lives.

This can even be a problem when we receive praise that has not been sought due to the good results of some action we have undertaken for God's glory. The Bible does not say we are to renounce such acknowledgement. It actually would seem that at times, such praise is God's way of affirming our obedience to what He has asked us to do. Sometimes when we think the whole world is beyond hope, it is a good thing to recognize that good can still be done in the world. I know it may sound contradictory, but the Bible does seem to indicate that when our motivation is to please God, not men, there is a healthy way to take into consideration respect for the opinions of other people. The issue becomes one of how we value such opinions and how we seek to use our influence for the Kingdom. At times, such praise of our actions can actually bring glory to God. Of course, the catch in all this is the danger of allowing such to happen and then unconsciously allowing that old love of praise for self to rear its ugly head. Pride and self-love are never very far from the heart of all we do.

This is the same spirit with which we are to treat money. The acquisition and pursuit of material wealth is never to be our primary motivation. But when God sees fit to prosper us in this area, we are to seek to use wealth for the glory of God and realize how seductive it can become. We must fight the battle against gaining wealth as an end in and of itself instead of keeping our mind set on the fact that wealth is only a means to an end. Wealth is a highly dangerous possession. Too easily does it become a way to increase our own comfort and luxury instead of a tool to help those who suffer, and by so doing bring glory to God.

In the previous examples, we see the principle at work that a relationship with Christ is not intended to extinguish our personal desires but rather to bring them under control as they are submitted to His lordship over our lives. In so doing, we reject the admiration of men to pursue a higher and better recognition that comes from God. We put earthly wealth in its true perspective so that we may strive with all the capabilities God has given us to attain true wealth that never fades or rusts away. These objectives lead to a true ambition and the exercise of all we have been given by God. We will accomplish far more than we ever could have accomplished with mere human praise as our motivator and mere earthly wealth as our reward.

Having said all this, it is unfortunate that I have to point out that the value most cultural Christians place on praise and wealth in no way reflects what the Bible teaches about these subjects. For many men and women, the *inordinate* love of *worldly glory* is not an issue due to their inability to achieve it.[6] But there is a version of this love that infects the most common circumstances of life. Too many people love the admiration and flattery given under the most ordinary of circumstances. The great lengths we go to in order to protect it, and the bitter anger with which we respond when it is attacked, reveal the high regard we place on our reputations in the eyes of men. The idea that we might suffer the loss of the world's opinion of us, or face dishonor and disgrace, is unacceptable.

The result of this way of thinking is predictable. If the outcome of obedience to God leads us to a lower estimation in the eyes of our peers, we often choose reputation over obedience. When earthly reward is of the highest value to us and worldly shame is viewed as the greatest of all possible evils, we are prone to change the course of our obligations to God and seek a way to do them that avoids the natural consequences of taking a stand against the cultural norm. We seek to serve God in ways that enable us to keep earthly gain and avoid worldly disapproval. Or we simply quit attempting to serve God fully.

There are numerous ways this tendency is exhibited. For instance, notice how any talk about God is excluded from our normal conversations. See how we attempt to come across as having socially approved sensitivities toward certain issues instead of having the biblical attitude. Our behavior is so conformed to cultural standards that if we were put on trial as a Christian, the case might be dropped for lack of evidence.

I would be remiss if I did not address one of the most visible activities that is the product of holding the opinions of men in too high an esteem. I speak of the practice of dueling.[7] This is a practice that has been allowed to exist for too long in a Christian society.

The essence of the practice rests on the belief that a person's reputation is to be guarded at any cost and that a person's disgrace is to be avoided with the same fervor. There have been numerous attempts to demonstrate how inappropriate this practice is. Usually these are based on moral arguments against malice and revenge. What has been ignored is the very root problem leading to the practice. Dueling is a demonstration of the preference for the favor of man rather than the favor of God, in a situation that is *in articulo mortis;* that is, "to the death." It leads to an instant in which both the life of a fellow human being and our life are at stake—one in which we might find ourselves in the very presence of God, propelled there by an act that offends Him.

You might be thinking that because you have never been in a duel, you have not sinned. But you must remember that we are in relationship with a God who holds us accountable for our thoughts as well as our actions. If you hold the conviction that in the proper circumstances, you would resort to a duel for the sake of your name and honor, then, in the judgment of God, you are guilty of a sin. This is especially the case with dueling, as it is the only sin I am aware of that involves this disposition to commit the sin whenever the circumstances dictate it. Nearly all in the upper classes of England are guilty.

I know I have not completely covered this subject of the love of worldly esteem, even with all I have written. It would be impossible in the limited space available in this book to fully investigate the topic. Hopefully, enough has been said to make it a subject of close examination in our own lives. The high esteem in which many hold this principle cannot be vindicated by some lofty ideal. It is in reality a product of the lowest origins. It springs from selfishness and vanity. These combine themselves with envy and jealousy in order to create a quality that can lead to disaster as well as achievement. On the one hand, it motivates industry and excellence. On the other, it leads to war and the destruction of entire societies. Although its benefits have been lauded, its deficits have rarely been examined.

If you read the writings of certain Christian moralists, you will notice that this subject is avoided at all costs. The lack of comment leads one to the conclusion that they have made a sort of deal with the devil to maneuver around this problem so as not to stir up the cultural waters.

Of course, much of what is written by Christian moralists often lacks any reference to Christian morality. The value of the applause of the crowd is not only allowed but also often commended with too few qualifications. To love money is viewed as sordid, while to love praise is treated as the mark of an exalted nature. There seems to be little recognition that along with any positive outcomes produced by the pursuit of personal recognition, there are many disastrous outcomes. It is a dynamic that fills us with vain conceits, vicious passions and the tendency to set our affections on things that steal our hearts away from God. Too many quickly applaud the side of the principle that might cause good while ignoring the side that can cause disaster.

It is a distinct characteristic of authentic faith not to be satisfied with the mere outward appearance of good but to be just as concerned with the motives behind the action and with the need for purity of the inner person. Authentic faith recognizes that the desire for praise, and the false pride it produces, is a constant challenge that requires diligent monitoring. It is also a battle that a man or woman who possesses authentic faith knows cannot be overcome without divine assistance. He or she recognizes that everything in our outward environment, and even that part of our inner nature that still resists total obedience to God, fights to embrace anything that leads to self-glorification and works against our attempts at genuine humility. Such is the battle for the human heart.

To fight this battle, people with authentic faith recognize that they must avail themselves of all the resources God provides to resist this love of self that continually encroaches on their sacred space. These resources include a rigorous self-examination to reveal our own flaws. This provides a reality check that reminds us of our need for Christ. Another resource is the recognition that whatever strengths we possess over other men and women are gifts that have been given to us as expressions of God's purposes for our lives. Along with these attitudes, we must work hard to keep a realistic view of human praise and the value of being held in honor, knowing that they are not worth the effort many put into acquiring them. They just are not worth the trouble! The praise of man is fickle. It is often given to those who do not deserve it, and can just as easily be taken away as it was given.

Another check on this tendency is to form friendships with others who are also seeking to please God. Good men and women will provide a reality check both when what we have done is to be commended and when it is to be challenged. But even the feedback of good friends is not to replace the rigorous exercise of conscience. No one can really know the state of our hearts but we ourselves.

If we hold the esteem of good men loosely, it will help us to be even more cautious as to how to respond to the praises of the world at large. Again, the goal is to use those abilities we possess for the right purposes. We are to employ them for the advancement of God's plans and purposes. They are not ends in and of themselves but means to a higher end. This is why the empty praise of man is so ridiculous. Praise is given to the tool, not to the accomplishment of the task the tool was designed for.

When we make this approach our rule of thumb, we will seek to use all the positive qualities and abilities we possess to move the cause of good forward. The esteem the world gives us can be a way to open doors that might not open for others, who, for whatever reason, are not held in high esteem by the culture. The man or woman of faith who also is held in high esteem by society can help remove obstacles that stand in the way of the progress of truth. They are in positions in which they are able to speak against the things that damage the society and bring to light those people and actions that deserve recognition but might not have the social standing to attract it.

There is a responsibility that comes with such standing. Reputation is a valuable quality that is meant to advance the causes of faith and virtue. The person of faith must be ready to relinquish it in a moment if need be, but they also must jealously guard against throwing it away. They must avoid situations and actions that might diminish it. They must avoid crude humor, selfish anger, discourtesy and any action that blatantly disregards the norms of common civility. If a reputation is to be lost, authentic faith only willingly loses it when the loss is part of doing the right thing. By their behavior and positive character, they will disarm those who have created a straw man out of religion. If through faulty perception their character is attacked, they will seek to vindicate themselves with proper attitude, not haughtily or with pride. They do not defend reputation as an end in and of itself, but because it is a tool to do what God has called them to do. Keeping in mind the ultimate outcome of life in this world, they will be able to fight the good fight, knowing that the things the world values will one day count for nothing, while all that God values will last forever.

In the same vein, the true Christian knows that if he or she is to hold the favor of God above the favor of men, he or she will have to become indifferent to the dishonor and lack of esteem that might be encountered in practicing authentic faith. People of faith throughout the ages, and even Jesus Himself, were despised and rejected by the world. If someone happens to hold a position in which he or she is viewed as both credible and popular, that person must watch carefully that such opinions don't become more important than being Christ's man or woman. Realistically, it does not hurt to even rehearse how we might respond if popularity were to turn to disgrace for the cause of Christ.

The most effective way to keep all this in balance is to make the pleasure of God our overriding desire. Keeping focused on Christ makes both the praises and curses of man lose their intensity. Conscience will become more sensitive in the midst of the confusion permeating the culture. With this mind-set, we are able to rise above the fickle shifting of human opinion and stay steadfast in our commitment to the One who never changes.

When our lives are controlled by these kinds of principles, we are able to move in and out of the shifting uncertainties of life in the world and maintain the stability and peace God imparts to us. This is not an easy battle, and it is constant. The enemy is always at the gates, looking for a way to tempt us in this area. It is a tricky path that seeks to "let your light shine before men" (Matt. 5:16) while at the same time resists the desire for the approval of this same group.

The fight is won in the small things. We should not be deceived into thinking that we can toy with this attitude in little areas and yet be able to resist when the temptation is great. As we resist seeking the favor of men and avoiding their disapproval, we grow in our ability to see how this desire affects so much of who we are and what we do. Even when we find ourselves doing the right thing for the right motivation and resisting the evaluation others place on it, the esteem often given such behavior threatens to sneak up on us in the very act of rejecting it.

This very trap plagues cultural Christianity. Before you know it, all is done for the applause of others. Faith loses its vitality, and we lose the battle. Careful vigilance is required to be sure our hearts are right and our motives pure. The Holy Spirit will help us if we sincerely desire to stay in a proper relationship with God and to keep our hearts pure. Once more, let me emphasize that it requires much discipline, careful (almost jealous) watchfulness, and divine intervention to win this battle.

Operating as cultural Christians might lead us to become nice, friendly and even kind, but it rarely will enable us to promote the happiness or welfare of others without the applause or recognition of the crowd. The person of authentic faith will not only be motivated to seek the welfare of others, but will also be able to do it with genuine humility, joyfulness and love.

This difference is easy to discern. Humility is the key—not a false humility that is often displayed by cultural Christians who actually relish the praise and recognition of others for the smallest acts of charity, but an authentic humility that is so deeply rooted that it is almost oblivious to what others think about what we do. This humility seeks *not* to be noticed. It pursues a quiet oblivion. Love and humility are the marks of one who has learned not to seek the favor of men but rather the favor of God as their motivating principle. It is a principle that is so independent of what people think that it forms a perfect contrast to Epicurean selfishness, Stoical pride, and to Cynical brutality. It is a reflection of the very character of Christ Himself.

By now you are probably wishing that I would move on. Perhaps I have given disproportionate attention to this subject, but since it is such a prevalent problem in the higher classes of society, I have felt compelled to treat it at length. My hope is that the very length to which I have drawn out the discussion will itself prove helpful in dealing with such an important issue.

Section Four: *Faulty Thinking About "Good" Lives and "Good" Deeds as Substitutes for Authentic Faith*

There is another area in which cultural Christians have faulty thinking regarding authentic faith. It has to do with the role good deeds and living a so-called "good" life play in the spiritual life. The error has to do with placing the proverbial cart before the horse. By that I am referring to the erroneous belief that if you are good enough and practice good deeds, that in and of itself is adequate to earn the favor of God and make up for the lack of placing God and His will first in your life.

It seems that there is a prevailing belief that if a person is kind and sweet; sympathizing, giving and affectionate; meets the expectations of the duties society feels are appropriate; and above all this is viewed as a useful and productive member of the community, this somehow makes up for a lack of genuine spirituality.

Some will say that making a distinction between belief and action is mere semantics. They will argue that the objective of faith is to produce these very qualities and that their existence is evidence that faith is at work. It is true that in many men and women, the most basic duties of society and family cannot be performed apart from the enabling influence God creates in their lives. But in many cases, all these qualities exist without any shred of authentic faith.

The result is that in many cases there exists a failure to distinguish between morality and spirituality. This is a fatal error! It is a fact that is aggressively disputed most by those who happen to suffer from it. In many cases, the very argument is the evidence that the ones arguing it are ensnared by the error. Their arguments are often defenses against their own fears and justifications for not acting to seek to change the state of those who need spiritual help to rise to the level of common decency demanded by the culture. Although this argument might appear sound, it cannot be defended when compared with the clear teaching of the Bible.

It is rarely observed in such discussions that when we talk about "good" people, and "good" deeds, such people and their deeds only exist hypothetically. Even when such descriptions are applied to men and women who actually exist, the evaluation is often exaggerated. No one knows the true state of the heart of those who practice the common courtesies of society and appear to be people with true goodness. The outward conduct of a person does not always reveal the true state of the inner person. In some cases, the outward behavior can be a mask that hides a twisted and unrighteous person on the inside. Such a person's actions and behavior can be a kind of self-atonement to make up for inner realities that are not pleasing to God. The outer becomes an assumed character, not an inner reality. If we could see the inner reality, we might be appalled. In reality, these people might be cruel rather than loving and base rather than refined. Gentle in public, they might be tyrants at home where the true beast, restrained in public, is unleashed.

Even when these character traits are genuine, the people who possess them often lack the strength and resolve to maintain consistency in the face of difficulty and struggle. These men and women rarely have the internal fortitude to take a stand against popular vice. Because their actual character is weak, they will often find themselves involved in the very practices a man or women of genuine faith is required to reject and oppose. When push comes to shove, it becomes obvious that self-interest rises high above unselfish service. The opinion of the crowd becomes more important than sacrifice of reputation for that which is truly good.

These positive qualities are often fragile when not rooted in authentic faith. They become short-lived when maintaining them requires sticking it out for the long haul. When all is going well, an appearance of good character and virtue can survive. When we are healthy and young and surrounded by friends who hold the same values we do, virtue can be easy. But when tough times come, when our health fails, when our businesses are in financial difficulty, or when our dreams are crushed, virtue can fade with the shifting of fate. Where does such virtue take us when the uncertainties of life turn against us? How does it hold up when the very friends who admired our goodness have left us behind because our fortunes have suffered reversal? Only then is true character tested for authenticity. And only then will authentic faith produce the results needed to make it through difficulty without compromising our character.

When disappointments come, anger replaces kindness in the hearts of superficial Christians. Encounters with the selfishness of humanity crush the warmth and affections they seemed to possess in easier times. They become harsh and selfish themselves. The once benevolent youth becomes a harsh and cruel tyrant; the joyous, generous young person turns sour, sullen and cold.

In the same way, those who are viewed as constructive members of society show their true colors when circumstances turn against them. That which was viewed as exceptional creative energy turns out to have been overrated. It turns out that these individuals' natural disposition has led them to usefulness. The satisfaction their efforts give them and the applause of the crowd more than repay them for what they have done. On the other hand, when you see men and women who have struggled under the most oppressive of backgrounds, without the advantages many in the middle and upper classes enjoy, giving all the effort they possess to do something positive for other people and society as a whole, you can probably assume they have experienced a genuine encounter with Christ. Their faith makes their accomplishments possible, even in the face of adversity.

What is good is only a matter of opinion in secular society. Using society's own standards of goodness, careful observation of the bigger picture may reveal that a particular good has been outweighed by general evil. When a society defines its own morality and then applies it to itself, that society can justify its own serious breaches of character. It is able to lower the standard to the detriment of all.

Even in the best of cases, the fundamental problem still exists that the motivation for life is still man-centered instead of God-centered. Goodness is no substitute for devotion. In its culturally defined forms, goodness can exist where love of God and passion for His glory do not. There is this mistaken notion that somehow God has a set of scales and our efforts in the areas we see as good need to balance our former actions that were bad. If the good outweighs the bad, we assume we are righteous. This is not the gospel. Such a belief always leads to a sense of false confidence. It is the product of faulty thinking and a lack of understanding of what the Bible teaches.

The argument that positive behavior is the equivalent of true faith is completely contradictory to the clear teaching of the Bible. As we have previously seen, the unequivocal teaching of the Bible is that there is no substitute for the love of God being our highest purpose. It is the height of arrogance to attempt to twist this teaching into one in which the efforts of humans are placed on par with a wholehearted love of God. This thinking comes from a form of mental gymnastics so distorted that I prefer not to spend the time refuting it. It is conceived in the resources of a mind that seeks to escape the convictions it is unable to stand before and to evade the obligations it cannot perform.

Hannah More has written, "Christianity is a religion of motives and principles."[8] God is concerned about the heart as well as the outward action. Only an action motivated by love of God is truly a Christian action. Even earthly fathers look for a proper attitude to accompany their children's actions. Proper action performed with poor attitude does not please us as parents. Neither does it please God.

The problem, of course, is that we cannot see into the heart of another. This means that the only way we have of evaluating the validity of another person's faith is by the actions he or she exhibits. When it comes to human evaluation, this is our limitation. But when it comes to God's evaluation, we are dealing with One who does have the ability to see into the human heart and weigh its motives. Somehow we become confused about this. We act as if God doesn't care about motive as long as the action is correct.

Although we have argued that correct action can be done without proper motive, the fact is that rarely will actions not suffer when the motivation behind them is false. We tend to work harder and better when our motivation is proper. When we act only out of a sense of duty, that which is done often reveals this defect.

We have all heard the comparison made of the nonbelieving man or woman who reflects a naturally positive and friendly character with the man or woman of faith who is so offensive by nature that we would prefer the company of the former to that of the latter. There certainly are instances when this is true. But why do we never hear of the contrast between people of faith who exhibit the character of Christ and unbelieving people who couldn't care less about character? I believe we would find the overwhelming evidence would fall in favor of the positive impact authentic faith has on the character of the one possessing and practicing their faith.

We should all remember that some people seem to have sunny dispositions by nature while others struggle with life. For the latter, the outward expression of the Christian faith can be a great challenge. Without knowing the struggles they brought into a life of faith or of how much their character has been changed from what it was before, we might judge such people harshly.

If you feel this about yourself—that your life does not reflect the reality of Christ in the way it should—do not lose heart. God is in the transformation business. Once your life has been invaded by the divine presence, He is able to change you from the inside out. The very fact that you struggle to be a person who reflects Christ's character is a sign that your faith is authentic. Don't give up. Don't become weary of attempting to be the man or woman God calls you to be. Keep a sharp eye on your behavior and never attempt to take the easy way out. Self-deception is one of the great enemies of a practical faith. That is why it is often helpful to have relationships with other Christians who can give you an accurate appraisal of the true state of your life. Let the Bible be your mirror. When it instructs you to be humble, kind, gentle or meek, the Holy Spirit can reveal whether you are or are not fulfilling such commands. Work hard to be an example of the power of Christ creating His character in you. When you do, you help advance the cause. Fight the good fight.

In the same way, keep a careful eye on the world around you. You will see that in general, it is a cruel and inconsiderate place. Try to see it through the eyes of faith. The need is immense; the danger is imminent. This understanding should move us to compassion and action. This inner and outer awareness can be a useful tool in your progress toward true Christian character. It is a wonderful sight to see a man or woman who through the years has been transformed by the work of the Holy Spirit. As Virgil said, "We marvel at fresh leaves and fruits not our own."[9]

I hope I have not given you the false impression that where good deeds exist without godly motivation, they are without merit. That is not what I intended at all. All such endeavors are good things. But such endeavors do not earn favor from God. The public praise and recognition that come from such actions is their reward in full. The acts of true faith flow from a heart devoted to God that continually is governed by the desire to know and do His will so that, ultimately, He will be glorified. Whatever action is done, regardless of how noble, that does not originate from this motivation is not Christian. I don't say this so that you judge the actions of others. I say this so that you judge your own actions and determine by what motivation your actions are produced. This will help keep you from slowly falling into the trap of actually believing the praise you receive. It is too easy to start out with the right motivation and slowly be seduced into doing things for the applause of man.

This is the tightrope we walk. On the one hand, we want our lives to be productive and effective; on the other, we don't want to lose the spiritual focus that is at the heart of our faith. I don't have the time to go into great detail on this balancing act, and I have to admit that I myself have not found any magic formula for achieving this balance in my own life. But because it is a subject of such importance, I will attempt to make a few comments about it.

What do you do when you sense you are losing your focus and slipping into action without passion? Are you getting too enmeshed and consumed with the affairs of the world? Or are you too engaged in pursuing some worldly object? First, you need to stop and take inventory. Take an honest look at the state of your heart and the situation you find yourself in. Ask God to show you the true state of things. If you find that in fact you are pursuing wealth or reputation and that your mind tends to be always occupied with such things, and if you find that success in attaining them gives great joy while disappointments in their acquisition distresses you, then you have a problem! Your heart has been captured.

When this happens, it is important to look at what you are trying to accomplish or acquire. Are you after the wrong thing? Because it is so easy to get caught in self-deception, check this with a few close friends. If you are unwilling to do this, it should be a signal that something is wrong. When you become aware of this, begin to distrust yourself. You will begin to look for all kinds of justifications to defend what you are doing. As you do, you will also find that your passion and valuation of the things of God will diminish.

When you find no fault in your conduct yet have a sense that something is wrong, you need to stand back and take a look at the bigger picture. Is there some area of your life that is out of conformity with what you know God wants? Have you been negligent of the spiritual disciplines of prayer and reading the Bible? Have your times of devotion been irregular or infrequent? Do you find such times being constantly interrupted? Have you fallen prey to the erroneous idea that you are too busy to give adequate time to these exercises, forgetting that the neglect of them usually results in less effective work time, while the exercise of them makes us more productive in the long run? It doesn't take long to see the effects of such negligence. It might be time to take inventory.

When taking stock, ask if the objects or achievements you are striving for are truly the things you believe God has called you to accomplish. If you believe they are, consider whether you might be giving them more time than they really require so that you lose the time you need to take care of your spiritual needs.

If, after careful examination, you reach the conclusion that you are on a proper course in both the object and energy of your activities, at least try to pursue them without giving as much of your heart to them as you have been giving. Attempt to practice the presence of God in the midst of the execution of the task at hand. This will give the enterprise a more spiritual tone.

Above all, guard against the temptation to conform your mind to the level that would justify your behavior. Keep your standards high! Recognize that without God's help, you won't be able to achieve them. Such awareness keeps us in the place where we need to pray consistently. It also creates a healthy level of humility that is so necessary to reflect the character of Christ.

The benefits of approaching our lives in this manner are numerous. Distress can be replaced by a sense of comfort and confidence, not in ourselves, but in God. The agitation we have experienced in our inner life can be replaced by peace. We might end up doing the same task or seeking to acquire the same object, but now we have moved back into an inner space where once again we are doing it all for the glory of God.

It is worth noting that in this entire endeavor, there is a subtle danger for the person who has a natural character that outwardly seems more Christlike. Ironically, it is this person, rather than the one who struggles to exhibit Christian behavior, who is actually more likely to allow self-motivated behavior to become a substitute for God-motivated behavior. If these natural behaviors were submitted to the cause of Christ, they would be wonderful. But when they are not so submitted, they actually become a danger to the one who possesses them. The person may fall prey to society's generous recognition of their goodness.

The truth is that when such character is not rooted in a spiritual foundation, it is flimsy and shaky at best. It will not withstand the pressures that the same actions, generated by authentic faith, can bear. When circumstances become difficult, these people don't stay the course. Their goodness was all a pretense, not a reality. In the end, authentic faith, not human goodness, will produce the greatest well-being of a society.

Section Five: *Other Problems with Cultural Christianity*

In our discussion of cultural Christianity, so far we have looked at the basic errors cultural Christians have about the true nature of authentic faith. We have also seen some of the consequences created by this faulty thinking. Before I move on to other subjects, I feel the need to make a few more observations about areas in which cultural Christians do not live in conformity with what the Bible teaches.

In the first place, in everything we know about cultural Christianity, there appears to be an inadequate understanding of true guilt and the evil of sin. Everywhere we look we see Christian faith reduced to a set of rules and regulations meant to police behavior. The result is that rather than having an understanding of sin gained from the Bible, the idea of sin is usually shaped in terms of the impact specific sins have on society. Everyone can see that murder, theft, fraud and some types of lying are problems impacting society in negative ways. Consequently, these sins are given more weight on the moral scale than sins such as idolatry, immorality, foul language, lewdness, pride, wrath, malice or revenge.

Often, these vices are condemned when exhibited by people from the lower classes because they are viewed as further degrading the lives of the poor and underprivileged. But when people of wealth and position exhibit these vices, they are excused as the natural expression of their prosperity or as an excess of their sense of humor. This observation has been confirmed by the writings of such scholars as Adam Smith, who obviously did not come to his conclusions on the basis of religious grounds.[10]

I'm sure someone will argue that the former class of vices are more easily recognized as damaging to society and are therefore easier to regulate by means of law. But what do people really think? Do they recognize the serious nature of the latter class of vices and stand against them as rigorously?

Even our language gives us away. We have invented terms to downplay the danger of certain vices by calling them freethinking, offbeat, jocular, edgy, and the like. We have no such way of describing murder, theft or fraud. These crimes are not so funny, and they obviously harm people. There is no "cute" murder or "offbeat" fraud. But there is edgy sexuality or offbeat humor. We clearly have established two separate classes of offenses.

In the one case, we explain away the offenses as having been spontaneous or a temporary failure to resist temptation. But in the case of the more serious crimes, one single failure is enough to be taken to court. The person who commits such offenses is labeled for life as a murderer, liar or thief. But when it comes to vices that are committed against God, we have no such strict guidelines. We apply a kind of creative logic. An individual can commit some of these actions repeatedly and still be deemed a Christian. We might even decide that even though this person's conduct is at times suspect, he or she is still a good Christian.

In the Bible, actions are evaluated by a much more rigid standard. You will never read of a "little" sin. There are no "white" lies. Take the Sermon on the Mount as an example. You do not find Jesus qualifying His comments based on the social standing of the members of His audience. If anything, Jesus warns the more privileged that they are in greater danger due to the temptations to which wealth exposes people. When you examine how Jesus dealt with these issues, you will see that idolatry, immorality, drunkenness and the like were dealt with in the same manner as theft and murder. Even Paul points out that those who continue to live like this "will not inherit the kingdom of God" (Gal. 5:21).

The problem that we see in our time is that because there is so little reverence for or sense of the holiness of God, we have no basis on which to take sin seriously. It is the understanding of the greatness of God that creates in the human heart the desire to please Him in all things and tries not to offend Him in any-thing. Such an attitude knows no arbitrary levels of offense. This is why such an attitude is called "the beginning of wisdom" in the Bible (Ps. 111:10; see also Prov. 1:7).

Sin is viewed in the Bible as rebellion against the rule of God in our lives. Persistent sin is evidence that we are not really in a proper relationship with Him. To those who take matters of faith lightly, this makes no sense. The Bible indicates that they have a big shock coming when Christ returns! It could not be clearer: Evil will be punished and true righteousness rewarded.

I must point out that these teachings in the Bible are not merely taught as the punitive result of God acting as a judge. They are often described as being the natural consequences of the bad choices we make. There is a system of cause and effect at work in the universe. It is woven into the very fabric of creation. The universe is moral by nature. It is a universe in which we are told God has a kingdom and Satan has a kingdom. Every person living on the earth belongs to one of these two kingdoms.

When we possess authentic faith and have sincerely surren-dered to Christ as Lord, we pass out of the kingdom of darkness and into the kingdom of the Son God loves (see Col. 1:13).

When we love the things God has given—His book, His special day, service done for Him—we demonstrate that something has already changed in who we are, even before the second coming of Christ. We are promised that what has already begun will one day be completed.

On the other hand, those who practice evil are called the children of their "father, the devil" (John 8:44). Their actions are referred to as his works, or his deeds. When we live like this, we are said to be subjects of his kingdom. If this is where we find ourselves, we can know that his destiny is ours as well. Jesus will say, "Depart from me, you who are cursed, into the eternal fire prepared for the devil and his angels" (Matt. 25:41).

If these statements do not strike terror in your heart, at least they should motivate serious apprehension about your destiny. Unfortunately, our minds seem to come up with the most amazing mental gymnastics to avoid dealing with these clear statements. We attempt to paint God in such a way that He could never be so harsh. This was the same error made by Adam and Eve in the Garden.

It would be interesting to find out what the people who lived at the time of Noah would have said if they had heard the message that a flood that would destroy the whole world was coming. They might have imagined that God would not do such a thing, yet the flood came exactly when and how it was predicted. We are even told in the Bible that the flood is to serve as an example for us to take seriously. Not only does the Bible tell us of this event, but science is also a witness to the fact that at one time every continent on the planet was covered with water. Nature itself bears witness to the message of the Bible.

I can hardly ever read the conditions Christ attributed to the time of the flood without thinking of the parallels in our own time. The wickedness of humanity was represented as being great and prevalent. It was a time of selfishness and luxury. People were anti-religion and inconsiderate. It reminds me of many European countries today. Yet the warnings against such things seem not to have influenced the day-to-day business of their societies. Jesus said they were "eating and drinking, marrying and giving in marriage" (Matt. 24:38) right up till the day the flood came. The result? They were all destroyed.

There obviously existed in Noah's time faulty thinking about what it meant to be a true believer. There was, as in our own nation, forgetfulness about their relationship with God being the great business of life. You see, the stakes are high: heaven or hell. Our task is to so order our beliefs and lives that we are preparing for the former and not settling for the latter. It is not true that because we were born in a nation that is called Christian, we are by default true Christians. Rather than the burden of proof lying on the argument to prove we are not, the truth is exactly the opposite. We are called to examine ourselves to make sure we really are in the faith—the authentic faith. What does the evidence show? Are we following our conscience or justifying what is clearly wrong? Do we explain away what we cannot justify? Do we give too much credit for acts that are only minimally commendable? Do we fool ourselves into thinking that our habits of vice are only occasional acts? What does the evidence say?

It seems we have forgotten that our work as Christians is to attempt to live according to the pattern Christ gave us and under the influence and enabling of the Holy Spirit. If this is not the primary task of the Christian, then what is? Nominal Christians have no understanding of why the Bible pictures the spiritual life as a race or as warfare. They see no need to rid their lives of anything that might impede their progress in growing in faith and obedience. To become equipped with what Paul calls the armor of God has no meaning whatsoever to cultural Christians. They have no interest in developing a passion for the things of God or His service on Earth. If the truth were to be told, they probably think that Christianity is a future reward in Heaven that they receive in return for having endured certain religious expectations here on Earth.

But this is all cultural Christianity, not authentic faith. In contrast to authentic faith, it is like a child's drawing compared with a painting by Rembrandt. It would be accurate to say that "Christianity" is a spiritual term, not a geographical one. It is a condition or a state that possesses certain qualities and attributes, not simply the result of living in a Christian country.

Further, Christianity is not a condition or state that anyone can be born into. There is no such thing as being born a Christian. To become a Christian, you must be newly created from within and experience a second birth. You cannot inherit a Christian nature; it must be created within you by the work of the Holy Spirit. It becomes our job to then exercise spiritual discipline to "work out [your] salvation" (Phil. 2:12). Even the apostle Paul spoke of how he applied all his energy and resources to this end.

When true Christians become aware of this challenge, they set out with focus and diligence to be sure they don't miss out on anything God has planned for their lives. They execute their spiritual duties as if they had escaped a country that was ravaged by the plague. It is not enough for them to simply cross the border; they exert all their energies to get as far away from the plague as possible. Knowing that the journey of faith will not be easy, they do not become discouraged when difficulties come. Knowing an adversary will oppose their efforts, they are not surprised or unprepared when the enemy attacks. As they set out on their way, they expect the early going to be difficult, but they know that the end of the journey will be great.

It is not without merit that those who pursue authentic faith in this manner are called pilgrims and strangers. A pilgrim is one who is on a journey. When the journey transcends his normal borders, he becomes a stranger. He is like a businessman who is sent into a new territory with the task of executing his job with diligence and tenacity and then returns home as soon as possible. Whatever pleasures he enjoys along the way, he enjoys with moderation. He is thankful when the weather is pleasant but is not diverted from his task when storms come.

He is a traveler. He expects the unexpected. But as he travels, he knows he is traveling to "a better country" (Heb. 11:16). He can observe the practices of this strange land and associate with its inhabitants. He even attempts to speak their language and where appropriate adopt their fashions, but he makes sure that he is not sidetracked or delayed along the way from accomplishing what his master has sent him to accomplish. He has business to which he must attend. He knows there will be temptations and distractions. He knows the enemy wants to delay and derail his advancement. This means that he must maintain his focus and direction. To make sure he is on the right track, he needs periodically to stop and take stock. Is he traveling in the right direction? Has he become distracted? Often he has the sense that he is making good progress. At other times he feels as if he is getting nowhere. All the passions of life are experienced along the way.

I hope you can see that this pilgrimage is impossible and unimaginable for the cultural Christian. This is no dreary duty! This is challenge and excitement. This is the ultimate adventure. This is what life was meant to be. From Pascal to Sir Francis Bacon, the travelers on this path have seen the end and found the journey more than worth making.

When we looked at the characteristics of the nominal Christian, we saw that the underlying deficit was a lack of the love of God. Many examples were pointed out, and the most cursory observation of these men and women makes it obvious. We know what love of God looks like. It is obviously missing in the majority of nominal Christians. The most blatant evidence is that they find no delight in either the service or the worship of God. Whatever outward actions they make in the name of religion are done as if slavishly performed for a harsh master. They are cold and sullen when it comes to things of faith. To the almighty Sovereign of the universe, who has given them life and new life, they give a dull, artificial and heartless kind of recognition, devoid of any gratitude for who He is and what He has done on their behalf.

Contrast this sentiment to the very first of the commandments. God tells us that our first duty is to love Him with all our hearts, minds, souls and strength (see Mark 12:30). This one emotion acts like a master spring that sets all the other components of the human heart into action. When it is present, many of the questions asked about what is appropriate and not appropriate behavior for a Christian would not even need to be asked. Rather than trying to figure out what they can get away with and how close to the line they can get, men and women would be attempting to discern what they could do to express their love for God. The motivation would be totally different, and we can only assume that the product would be also. Love avoids all that might harm the beloved and seeks out all that might be pleasing.

I know I am about to tread on delicate soil, but I feel compelled to apply this principle to the way we entertain ourselves. It has been asked whether certain kinds of entertainment are appropriate for Christians. What would our response be if in every case we evaluated our decisions about our leisure pursuits by asking if our choices would demonstrate our love for God? Is there any way that we would engage in immoral or inappropriate kinds of activities when we are attempting to honor God and serve Him?

When entertainment is crude or off-color, the answer seems too obvious. When actions we would never allow in our normal interactions of daily life are part of some form of entertainment, something is wrong. The very values we seek to influence in a positive direction are intimately woven into the fabric of much of what passes for entertainment today. Much of the content of popular entertainment contains elements the Bible expressly forbids. Somehow, when it comes in the form of entertainment, we find it less offensive. In reality it is all the more dangerous. We often let our guard down when engaging in certain types of entertainment. I fear we have been conditioned to accept such things in much the same way that a frog learns to accept ever-warming water, until eventually it is boiled to death without even noticing the change in temperature. Such is the influence of the entertainment industry in our time.[11]

If the love of God is not extinct in the majority of professing Christians, it is certainly at an all-time low. Even our love of our fellow man is not at the level we would like to pretend it is. Our country is filled with institutions designed to help other people, and these institutions are pointed out as examples of how well we care about our fellow human beings.

I believe this praise is exaggerated in the case of these institutions. Nominal Christians love to draw attention to the external evidence such institutions provide. They would have us believe that the very existence of the institutions is proof of the good will toward their fellow man held by the members of the higher or wealthier classes in this country. But do these institutions give proof of the internal benevolence of those who have funded them? Is the internal motivation the same in this time of prosperity and abundance as it would be if the economy were struggling and these same benefactors needed to give out of their means instead of their surplus? What are we to think when philanthropy is not the product of concern for the poor? What if it comes at no real cost to the philanthropist? Often these givers are simply using the same approach to giving money that they used in accumulating large sums through means of greed.

How would these same men and women score were they to be tested by the Bible's standard of appraising authentic philanthropy? How is giving to be evaluated when it comes from a source filled with pride, vanity, self-love, self-interest, love of ease or of pleasure, ambition and love of social position? The Bible tells us that "God loves a cheerful giver" (2 Cor. 9:7) and that He is looking for the one who gives out of self-sacrifice rather than without any measure of personal cost. The bottom line seems to be whether we are willing to give even when it really costs us. In the same way, are we willing to do the right thing when doing so might actually result in the loss of personal prestige or human praise? It again all boils down to what is happening in our hearts when we take actions that outwardly are viewed as humanitarian and philanthropic. Are our actions lavish expressions of our love for God or simply half-hearted actions taken because of social expectation?

When evaluated by these criteria, I fear that the majority of professing Christians have done little that would merit the praise of heaven. Rather than congratulating ourselves on our benevolence, we need to realize that we continually fall short of the giving spirit that comes from true love of God and man. In the end, the standard we are called to measure our giving against is the giving nature of God Himself. Jesus told us that we are to be perfect, as the Father is perfect. When that becomes our criteria and our measuring rod, it reduces all of us to a healthy humility. This kind of thinking is virtually unknown among cultural Christians.[12]

Section Six: *The Big Problem with Faulty Thinking About Christian Theology*

At the risk of repeating myself, all of the defects of the practitioners of nominal faith in our day can be traced back to the radical misunderstanding or lack of understanding they possess of the distinctive doctrines of the faith they profess: the true state of human nature—the truth of what Christ accomplished on the cross—and the transforming influence of the Holy Spirit. Right here is the watershed between the faith of nominal Christians and those who practice the faith that Christ came to make possible. The difference is so critical that I will attempt to further illustrate the problem.

There are those who have never given serious consideration to Christ and have spent their lives drifting along with the culture's ideas of the good life. Then, through some circumstance, these people experience a wake-up call about their faith. Maybe they have contracted a serious illness or experienced the sense of loss that comes when a friend or loved one dies. It could be that they experienced a reversal of fortune that awakened them to the reality of the precarious nature of life. Whatever the reason, they begin to look for some source of meaning in their lives that will give them a more stable foundation. In their search, they become aware that they have offended God by the way they have lived. With this sense in their minds, they set out on a course of personal reformation.

Right at this point we see the tragedy of the common understanding of cultural Christianity. These men and women might desire to change, but they don't have any understanding of what their real problem is or of the only solution that is able to address it. They might be aware that they need to make some changes in their behavior and give up something they are doing, and they even might have the idea that they should get involved in religion. But lacking the sense of the radical problem of spiritual death and the knowledge of the solution for this condition that only the work of Christ provides, they attempt to fix things by means that never work. As Shakespeare once observed:

They do but skim and film the ulcerous place,
While rank corruption, mining all within,
Infects unseen.[13]

It is not unusual for these men and women to fall back into the habits they were previously enslaved by and to deceive themselves into thinking that the small changes in behavior they have made have fixed the problem. They might even assume that what they have done makes them Christians. It doesn't take long for them to realize, however, that at some level their performance does not match the standard Christ has set for His followers. Unable to hit the mark, they tend to lower the standard. Once they have reached a place where their behavior meets the new requirements or vice versa, they settle into a state of contented complacency regarding the issues of authentic faith.

Others go farther than this. If they have come to grips with some sense of the coming judgment and the serious business of sin, they strive with all their effort to correct their behavior. Over and over, they fail to meet the standard that they sense they must reach. Finally, in total frustration they simply give up and quit trying. Sometimes in their despair, they give in to the former temptations, seeking some kind of comfort from the very actions that have led to their sense of defeat. Or, again out of despair, they might attempt to change their thinking and argue against the demands of authentic faith, never really believing what they are arguing about. These are men and women who are pursuing the right goal but have mistaken the way it can be accomplished. *The path they are now pursuing is not the one made possible by the work of Christ and will not lead them to the life they are desiring nor the peace for which they crave.*[14]

They will turn to ministers and counselors to get help with their spiritual instruction. If these helpers have embraced the prevailing religious system in our country, they will lead those in need astray by assuring them that as long as they really try to do the right thing, they have nothing to worry about. These ministers and counselors might even teach those in need of instruction that they don't need to worry because Christ has died for their sins. These religious leaders will actually reinforce the faulty thinking that all they need to do is give it their best effort and trust that everything will come out all right in the end. It is much more advisable to read the works of those who actually understand the principles of true faith and diligently study how to enter into and live a life of authentic spirituality.

These men and women need to take seriously what the Bible and the Church teaches to those who find themselves in this dilemma. They need to study and grasp the entire foundation of their confessed faith. This would include recognizing that the awareness of their problem, and their desire to do something about it, are gifts from God to get them started on the spiritual journey. In response to this awareness, they are instructed to bow before the cross of Christ in true repentance and, turning from sin, place all their hope and confidence in the grace of God and the work of Christ to get them on the right track.

Believing in Jesus means we personally accept His work on our behalf and open our lives to His indwelling presence by the Holy Spirit. Those who are not familiar with the teachings of the Bible must come to terms with the statement that they are required to "believe in the Lord Jesus, and you will be saved" (Acts 16:31). Submission and dependence are the appropriate responses to the teaching of Jesus: "Remain in me, and I will remain in you. No branch can bear fruit by itself; it must remain in the vine. Neither can you bear fruit unless you remain in me. I am the vine; you are the branches. If a man remains in me and I in him, he will bear much fruit; apart from me you can do nothing" (John 15:4-5). All of it is a gift. As Paul says in the letter to the church in Ephesus, "For it is by grace you have been saved, through faith—and this is not from yourselves, it is the gift of God" (Eph. 2:8).

I imagine that some of you might think I am spending too much time emphasizing these facts, but to tell you the truth, I don't think it is possible to spend too much time on this subject. It is the central truth on which all of authentic Christianity rests. You cannot work your way to heaven. You cannot do anything to earn the grace or forgiveness of God. Your good behavior does not balance out the guilt of your sin. The great distinction between Christianity and cultural religion is that cultural religion believes all these things can be obtained by our own efforts. True Christianity is looking for something much greater. *True Christians look to God to restore the image of God to their soul but know that this is not something they are able to accomplish. All their hopes of attaining this rest on total reliance on the Holy Spirit who comes to indwell them when they open their lives to Jesus Christ.*

Notice the critical order here. Our change of behavior does not PRECEDE our reconciliation to God and somehow become the CAUSE of God's favor; it follows our coming into relationship with God and is its EFFECT! It is by FAITH IN CHIRST only that a man or woman is made right in the sight of God; is delivered from God's judgment and the hold of Satan; is adopted into the family of God; becomes an heir of God and a joint heir with Christ, entitled to all the privileges that belong to this high relation; is partially renewed to the image of the Creator in this life; and is totally renewed to the perfect likeness of Christ in the life to come, when we will experience God's eternal glory and love, forever.[15]

Having entered into this relationship, the true Christian then seeks to grow in his or her spiritual life by studying the Bible in order to understand the doctrines of the faith. In studying and contemplating the life of Christ, the true Christian attempts to model his or her behavior after that of Jesus. It is the neglect of study of the Bible and reflection on the life of Christ that is at the heart of the practical errors of the majority of confessing Christians. Mere morality is dwarfish compared to the results of true faith. Morality as an answer to the pitiful state of the human condition reveals a total misunderstanding of the enormous problem of the fallen human condition.

This is a problem so massive that God gave His Son to die on the cross to solve it. When we think we can atone for our sin by becoming good, it is like a slap in the face of Christ. The cold sense of obligation and the grudging attitude of any act of service that accompanies cultural Christianity is completely inconsistent with the fact that a true Christian "is the temple of the Holy Ghost" (1 Cor. 6:19, *KJV*) and that our response to Christ is to demonstrate that we have been "delivered from the power of darkness, and . . . translated . . . into the kingdom of his dear Son" (Col. 1:13, *KJV*).

All our behavior, as those who have entered into this union with Christ, is to flow from these biblical truths. These truths are to motivate us to serve God with joy, thankfulness and love. We are to be a people who live with the experience of eternal gratitude.

If we are going to walk worthy of Christ, we have to practice one central discipline. As the writer of Hebrews exhorts, we are to fix our eyes on Jesus. We are to run our race LOOKING UNTO JESUS as our motivation.[16]

This is the key. If we do this one thing, we will be unable to treat our faith in the superficial way most cultural Christians do in our time. They want to live their spiritual lives on their own terms. It doesn't work.

Looking unto Jesus!

It is in maintaining this focus that we realize how logical it is to make an unconditional surrender of our total beings to the will and service of God. If we truly are not our own, but have been purchased by God and belong to Him, then it makes sense to live with the passion to glorify God with all we are and in all we do. Can we hold back if we really understand this? Can we compromise our attitude and response to sin without immense shame? We can only do this if our hearts are dead to any response to these things.

Looking unto Jesus!

When we fix our gaze on Jesus, we see in the most vivid colors how hateful sin is to the perfect holiness of God. Rather than sin going unpunished, God gave His only Son and allowed Him to suffer for our sin. It takes unthinkable vanity to believe that God will not treat unrepentant sin harshly when we see what it cost Him to provide forgiveness.

Is it any wonder that hell, described in Matthew 8:12 as a place of "weeping and gnashing of teeth," is the alternative to a positive and grateful response to the One who existed from all eternity in a relationship of perfect equality with the Father and yet was willing to humble and empty Himself of that glory to become incarnate and die the horrendous death of a common criminal so that He might provide a way for us to escape such a place?

Looking unto Jesus!

It is this focus that helps us grow in the love of God. Here we see the certainty of His love for those who will turn to Him. Here love is demonstrated. Here is the basis for a reciprocal affection. While we steadily gaze at the cross of Christ and contemplate the wonder of it all, unless our minds and hearts are dead, will we not respond with hope, trust, joy and overflowing gratitude? We will maintain an attitude of attempting to please God in all things, knowing that any efforts toward that end will be lovingly accepted. We will desire to stay in a place of favor with God, and that very desire will assure us that we are. Whenever we become conscious that we have done something to offend Him, we will be truly sorry and place our offense under the finished work of the Cross so that we may immediately renew our fellowship with the Lord. Our very failure will serve to renew our desire not to offend Him in the future. It is probably unnecessary to point out, but all these attitudes and desires are the elements of a relationship of love. All this, then, is the logical outcome of a firm grasp and understanding of the great truths of the faith.

I have already said much about the love of our fellow man. It is obvious that this is the duty of a true Christian. It needs to be said, though, that it is at the foot of the Cross that we receive great motivation to treat each other this way. From the Cross, we still hear the Savior say, "As I have loved you, so you must love one another" (John 13:34). We share with all humanity the common experience of being desperately in need of God's love and forgiveness and of being totally unable to do anything apart from receiving it with open arms on the merit of what Jesus has done. It is this that moves us to view our fellow brother or sister as objects of our compassion and care. The uncaring spirit of the world around us further motivates us to help those in need. The small injuries we suffer in the course of our human experience fade in comparison to the suffering Jesus endured to forgive our sin and make new life possible. Our contemplation of the Cross softens our hearts toward others. We desire to treat others as He has treated us. This desire drives us to take action that will express His love.

Looking unto Jesus!

As we fix our gaze on Jesus, we see the model of true humility. The work of redemption is a constant reminder that it was our fallen condition and helplessness that required His passion. Such knowledge makes us remember our true state and our unworthiness of all Christ has done on our behalf. There is no place for pride or an inflated sense of self-importance when our gaze is fixed on Jesus. The way others treat us is not nearly as important as we feel it to be when our focus is not on the self.

We grow less irritable, less dissatisfied, more soft, more courteous and gentle. When our service to Him results in poor treatment of ourselves, we realize that nothing we encounter is even close to the great humility He displayed during all that He suffered. At the same time, the Bible assures us that the power of the Holy Spirit that is now at work within us, made possible by the death of Christ, is responsible for any success we experience in our endeavors to improve in virtue. The conviction of this truth does wonders to curb our natural tendency toward vanity. All growth in grace will likewise result in growth in humility.

Looking unto Jesus!

The writer of Hebrews reminds us that Jesus "endured the cross, despising the shame," for us (v. 2, *KJV*). The solemn contemplation of that scene should produce within us the kind of attitude it takes to be a true servant of Christ here on Earth. It reminds us that life is short—eternity is forever! When we have this attitude about life, it enables us to take the things that really count more seriously and to give the trinkets and vanities of the world their proper place of priority. Sex, money and power lose their stranglehold on our lives. Even the wholesome things of the temporal world that we hold dear take on a different shade of importance. We gain a divine point of view on life that helps us reevaluate earthly success in order that we might pursue a success that comes from above. The cultural evaluation of our lives is inconsequential to us. Even when despised or degraded, we are not shaken. When life hands us difficulties, we are not ruffled and we do not become irritated. We look at the bigger picture, and looking to the Cross, our small difficulties become less of a problem than the luxuries and comforts we enjoy that have become an expected way of life.

In these moments of clarity, we are reminded that Jesus possessed little, yet He never complained. And if we find ourselves in circumstances of greater difficulty than the normal ups and downs of daily life, we deal with these difficulties through the filter of our vision of Christ on the cross. What He suffered for our benefit outweighs almost anything we must deal with. We face challenges and difficulties as part of God's plans and purposes for our life, knowing that in the midst of difficulty, He is there. We have confidence that even though we might not understand everything that happens to us, God will work all things out in a way that accomplishes His purposes. If this means we go through disappointment, illness, shame or poverty, we are able to trust Christ. He is the One who went before and will bring us through. In ways beyond comprehension, there is a sense of God's grace and peace in the midst of difficulty.

Looking unto Jesus!

We are called to fix our gaze on Jesus, the originator and the One who brings all things to completion, who endured the shame and suffering of the cross for the greater goal of the joy the Father offered (see Heb. 12:2). We look beyond the suffering of the cross to the glory Jesus now enjoys, having once again taken His place in the presence of the Father. There in His glory, His concern is ever for our progress in our relationship with Him. Hebrews even tells us that He always intercedes on our behalf before the Father (see 7:25). When we recall these truths, our hearts are refreshed and our spirits revived. When life is tough, we look beyond the seen to find our courage in the things that are unseen. When our faith is firm, danger, opposition and outright attack do not control our response. We live by faith. The worst the world throws at us can become the instrument by which, when the vessel is broken, the fragrant aroma of Christ is released. It is amazing that it is often in the darkest moments of our lives that the light of Christ shines the brightest.

Of course, it is all too rare that these are our actual responses to the difficulties life in a fallen world brings our way. Too often, it is the emotions of grief and confusion that surface during these times. Our response feels like a failure to reveal Christ and His reality in our lives.

When this happens, don't linger too long in your self-pity. Instead, get back in the action by getting on with God's business. Keep a close watch on your heart. Don't get entangled in immorality. Do the next indicated thing God seems to be leading you to do. Attempt to be an imitator of Christ in your behavior. His goal was always to do the will of the Father. Yours should be the same. Do justice. Show mercy. Be about the Father's business. Guard against the attacks of the enemy. Live like those who are eagerly waiting for the coming of the Lord Jesus Christ. Take inventory of how you are using your time, talents and resources. Live like you love Jesus! Do it with more gusto than the people of this age pursue fame, fortune and power.

As you go through your day, take mini "retreats." Think about God and the unseen things of His kingdom. Think about Jesus. Remember He is working on your behalf even as you entertain the thought. These are the small disciplines that keep us on task during the day. They put all we do into a proper perspective. And if these small moments of focus can keep us on track, think what it will be like when the realities we place our hope in are actually manifested! What a day that will be, when we see the risen Christ in all His glory return for those He has purchased by His blood. When all the pain, suffering and injustice of the world will be eliminated and every tear wiped from our eyes to be replaced by the fullness of joy that comes from living unhindered in His presence. On that day, we will join the host of heaven and worship God with the words John heard on Patmos: "Salvation belongs to our God, who sits on the throne, and to the Lamb" (Rev. 7:10).

So never forget that the main difference between authentic faith and the cultural Christianity that the majority of churchgoers in our country practice is primarily a result of faulty thinking about the core truths of the gospel. If understood at all, these truths are viewed by cultural Christians as unimportant to the actual practice of their faith. These truths have become mere curiosities often relegated to a time long gone that has nothing to do with the present. But to the men and women who possess authentic faith in Jesus Christ, *these truths are the center of gravity toward which all of life is in motion. They are the sun of their solar system! They are the origin of all that is excellent and lovely and the source of light and life!*[17]

The human mind cannot reason to these conclusions. Even the Old Testament is but a dim pointer toward their truth. But when you read the Gospels, your eyes are unveiled and you can see "the light of the knowledge of the glory of God in the face of Jesus Christ" (2 Cor. 4:6, *KJV*). And as we behold his glory, we are transformed so that we can reflect His glory in all we do and in all we are (see 2 Cor. 3:18). In the words of William Cowper:

You are the source and center of all minds,
Their only point of rest, ETERNAL WORD!
From you departing, they are lost, and rove
At random without honor, hope, or peace.
From you comes all that soothes the life of man,
His high endeavor, and his glad success,
His strength to suffer, and his will to serve.
But O Great Giver of all good,
You are of all your gifts, yourself the crown!
Give what you can, without you we are poor;
And with you rich, take what you will away.[18]

Notes

1. In the original text, Wilberforce does not give a title to this section.
2. Virgil, *The Aeneid*, bk. 6, lines 730-31.
3. Wilberforce italicizes "servants" and "children" for emphasis.
4. In the original text, Wilberforce does not give a title to this section.
5. Juvenal, *Satires*, bk. 10, line 96.
6. Wilberforce italicizes these words.
7. Dueling was a common practice among the upper classes of British society during Wilberforce's time. Although the practice is foreign to us, the principles are timeless.
8. Hannah More, *Thoughts on the Importance of the Manners of the Great to General Society*, 1788.
9. Virgil, *Georgics*, bk. 2, 82.
10. Adam Smith was a great Scottish economist. The origin of this reference is unknown, although it may be an allusion to Smith's classic work *The Wealth of Nations*, published in 1776.
11. Wilberforce is specifically commenting on the English theater. He takes the position of Francis Bacon and John Witherspoon before him.
12. Wilberforce ends this section by going back to his discussion of the theater and focuses particularly on the damage done to female performers (prostitution was common in the theater during that time). He argues that in love, we should not promote anything that has such a negative impact on another human being.

13. William Shakespeare, *Hamlet*, act 3, scene 4, line 93.
14. Wilberforce italicizes this thought.
15. Wilberforce italicizes this entire section for emphasis.
16. Wilberforce will now repeat the phrase "Looking unto Jesus!" numerous times and with letters in bold type to reinforce his point.
17. Wilberforce italicizes this thought for emphasis.
18. Revised from William Cowper, *The Task*, bk. 5, lines 898-909.

CHAPTER FIVE

ARGUMENTS FOR TRUE CHRISTIANITY

The Superiority of Authentic Christian Faith,
Evidence of Its Divine Origin

Let me break away from the plan of action I have been following to point out several dimensions of Christianity that I find to be part of the beauty of authentic faith. Cultural Christianity does not offer these benefits, and those who are cultural Christians don't have the foggiest idea of what I am about to say. Although I am deviating from my original plan, I hope that when you understand what I am about to explain, you will see how these very features lend credibility to all I have written so far.

It is true that even a cursory examination of Christian faith will reveal the amazing things God has done to express His love. But when we take the time and effort to look closely at the marvelous intricacies of true faith, we see an even greater beauty of the system. Let me return to the subject of the last chapter for a minute to demonstrate what I am talking about. There we saw how the central teachings of the Bible and the influence those teachings have on our practical lives exist in a perfect harmony that a casual glance at faith fails to apprehend.

I probably don't need to point out, but I will mention, that the same perfect harmony exists between the various elements of true biblical faith. This harmony begins with the foundation facts of our fallen human nature, the reconciled relationship with God that the work of Christ on the cross provides, and the restoration and transformation of our inner person by the presence and action of the Holy Spirit. The three are all parts of one whole and exist in unity and mutual congruence.

As true as this is with the foundations of faith, it is also the case with all the leading doctrines of Christian faith. They all fit together in a wonderful harmony that forms the foundation for a meaningful life, both now and in the age to come.

The actions and thinking most emphasized in the Bible as the goal of spiritual living are reverence and love of God; love, kindness and meekness toward our fellow human beings; a proper priority regarding the possessions and events of this life as compared to eternal things; and a healthy practice of self-denial and humility.

I have already pointed out the relationship between our attitude and heart toward God and how these impact our attitudes and behaviors toward other people. In particular, when you look closely at how certain dimensions of your character work together to promote and reinforce one another, you cannot help but come to the conclusion that they exist and operate in perfect harmony. This might be recognized from what has already been written, but I would like to take another quick look at this relationship. For instance, when you explore the actions of kindness and humility, you will see that the perfect foundation out of which these behaviors flow is the virtue of self-denial and moderation in your enjoyment of material possessions.

The chief reason people cannot get along together is that most are filled with pride and a distorted sense of self-importance. This in turn results in a demand for others to treat them the way they view themselves and leads to an unrealistic assessment of the value of material possessions and worldly honor. These dynamics produce a terrible competition between men and women to possess them. The rough edges of one person rub against the same in another and create a friction that is bound to disturb the waters of interpersonal harmony and peace.

When Christ is at work in our lives, He files down those rough edges. Instead of rubbing against each other, we work together like a well-oiled machine. When this is not the case, we have to wonder if we are seeing cultural Christianity instead of true faith. Cultural Christians might verbalize the need for love and benevolence, but their bondage to pride and self-importance keeps them from exercising these virtues and leads them to the pursuit of personal and professional success.

Some have mastered an outer appearance that enables them to pursue these goals while maintaining a veneer of goodness, but they lack any genuine love in their hearts. When the pressure is on, whether through disappointment or interpersonal strife, their true colors will show. They might have even mastered the art of disguising their hostility, but internally they are stewing. Their anger may break out at any minute if they let down their guard. This seems to be particularly true of those who have been elevated by our society because of success or notoriety. They have learned how to put on an appearance of goodness and respectability while they frantically pursue nothing but their own selfish interests. It is like people sitting at a card table. They might exhibit a good-natured attitude toward the others at the table, but internally they are hoping that the others will lose so that they might win. It is such a charade that you have to admire men and women of the working classes who never had the opportunity to learn so-called manners and who let you know exactly what is on their minds.

Authentic faith is not interested in being able to put on a virtuous mask. It demands truth in the inner person. The person of faith stands in the presence of the One who searched our hearts (see Ps. 139:1-4). The true believer attempts to live in an atmosphere of benevolence and works to avoid any action or thought that would distort or diffuse its purity. This is why placing ourselves in positions where we must compete for ascendancy over another person can be so damaging. It is hard to love someone with sincere love when you are exerting all your energy to rise above that person.

The instructions of the Bible that call us to put possessions and honors in their proper perspective help free us to love. They enable us to genuinely care for those who have been more successful by the world's standards, even if they have attempted to block our efforts to attain the same. When we keep our "minds on things above" (Col. 3:2), we have no reason to be envious or hostile toward those whose focus is on worldly fame and fortune.

The instruction of true faith to hold what others think of us with a very loose grip likewise frees us to love those who have attacked our reputation or falsely demeaned our character. A good barometer of the authenticity of our faith is how we respond to the attacks of those who treat us as if they are above us. True humility handles such treatment with grace. When we do not retaliate against those who offend us, we open the door to reconciliation with our adversary.

It is another virtue of authentic faith that moral achievement is valued more highly than intellectual achievement. It calls believers to pursue moral excellence more than knowledge. This stands in contrast to many of the so-called mystery religions that lead their followers to a so-called deeper knowledge that becomes the source of their salvation.

If you look at many of the major world religions, such as Hinduism or Islam, you will find different classes or levels of advancement based on the amount of information one has mastered. This obviously puts those in the lower classes, who might not have the ability to read, at a great disadvantage. The majority of mankind can never make much progress in these systems. Some ancient philosophers even advocated keeping the masses ignorant for the general good of the population. This suggests that the mass of humanity is an inferior breed from the higher, more educated elite. True Christianity operates in an exact opposite manner. Not only is the gospel intended for all humanity, but it also has a special place among the poor. It was even characterized by Jesus as "the good news preached to the poor" (Luke 7:22).

The emphasis true Christianity places on the preference of moral virtue over intellectual achievement has a value that supersedes the practical manner in which virtue fits the goals of the faith. It is a goal in which we have the ability to excel. Not all of us have the ability to achieve intellectual greatness, but we all can excel in the pursuit of virtue. Those who have made the pursuit of knowledge their passion are usually the first to acknowledge that their achievements have been moderate at best. Even if these people were not so candid, we would find evidence for this fact ourselves. It is among their ranks that we find multiple examples of weakness, shortsightedness and the tendency to make mistakes. The wisest and most learned are the ones who recognize the futility of any pride in human wisdom. It is usually the pseudo-intellectuals who play that game and hide behind this façade.

This is not the case in the pursuit of morality. Humanity was made in the image of God. Although we are fallen and that image has been distorted, there is still a part of the image of the Creator in every human being. It is this part of our being that can be renewed once again into conformity to the image of Christ (see Eph. 2). Because of Christ, we have the means available, not only to be forgiven, but also to be cleansed and renewed in our inner being. By the inner presence of Christ by means of the Holy Spirit, we are made capable of striving to attain real progress in our efforts to live the true Christian life. As we take advantage of the means God has provided to tackle this pursuit, we can have confidence that He will help us succeed.

I have known men and women who were living examples of this fact. Let me tell you about one friend who was a great example for me in this area.[1] He did not live a long life, but it was one filled with great labor. He made the world a better place by his life. His example motivates all who knew him to be more diligent in the pursuit of a life like his. I hope you don't think I am taking the other gifts God has given us or the outcome of human effort in other areas too lightly. But in all honesty, when compared to the bigger picture and the glory of God, the praise given all human achievement is like the praise we might give an ant for the load it is able to carry compared to its body weight. The feat might look impressive, but it has no great impact on the world in which we live. Such is our vanity. Our personal achievements are highly overvalued. This is not the case in the pursuit of our true dignity.

I also would like to point out that I am not attempting to give proof of the truth of Christian faith. Others much more qualified than I have done an admirable job at that task. Writers such as William Paley are owed a great debt of gratitude for the way in which they have taken the evidence on behalf of Christian faith and shown with great skill how it makes perfect sense.[2] Having said all this, I would like to point out one small feature of the faith that impresses me with particular force. This is the way that so many streams of support come together to create a case. A great number of writers have written of the variety of kinds of evidence that support the claims of Christ and Christianity. They have examined the proof from prophecy, from miracles, from the character of Christ, from the nature and excellence of the practical instructions of the faith and from the amazing way the doctrines of the faith complement the practical actions of the faith. Others have carefully examined the internal evidence of the Bible itself, as well as the early evidence of the reality of the faith in the lives of those who proclaimed it.

There are many lines of argument that have been brought forth in defense of the faith. The abundance of the evidence makes the arguments against Christianity seem irrational at best. So many different lines of proof, all so strong, coming together to establish the credibility of Christianity can hardly be explained except by the logic of its truth. I do not believe you could examine any other religious system in the world with such a multitude of approaches and find the consistency and clarity you find in real Christianity.

Notes
  1. Wilberforce is probably speaking of his friend Matthew Babington, who had recently died.
  2. William Paley was a great Christian apologist of Wilberforce's day.

THE CURRENT STATE OF CHRISTIANITY

How We Got Here, the Political Importance of This Condition, Ideas About These Facts

U p to this point, I have focused my comments on the state of those who are *professing Christians*. I would like to broaden my observations at this point to the *general state* of Christianity in the country.[1]

It has been repeatedly demonstrated throughout history that religious systems have existed that promote the well-being of political communities. This fact has been so undeniably evident and so well documented that I am not going to attempt to prove it true. It has been maintained, not only by scholars and clergy, but also by the most celebrated philosophers and politicians of every age.

Even if you do not particularly believe what Christianity claims, you would be hard pressed not to realize that it is a religious system that has produced untold benefits to the societies over which it has held influence. It is in this light that I again state that the spiritual condition of a country at any given time is an issue that has great political ramifications. In light of this relationship, it becomes extremely important that a society knows whether its spiritual underpinnings are in a state of decline or advance. If in decline, the society must determine if anything can be done to prevent a further slide.[2]

If the previous observations about the state of Christianity in our country are correct, you should become quite apprehensive about the impact these things might have on our political system. This apprehension should be even greater once you realize that authentic faith has been on the decline for quite some time now and continues to slide in that direction at the present moment.

When we attempt to evaluate the state of faith in a country at any given moment and then attempt to compare it to any previous period, we need to be very careful to avoid any mistakes that might skew the data. At any given point in the history of a society, there exists what you might call a general standard of accepted morality. The standard might vary in the society at different points in time and also among different classes of people within the society. When people fall below this standard (or rise noticeably above it!), they tend to fall into disfavor with the general population. This tendency serves to motivate men and women to seek that standard in their behavior. It follows that when this is the reason for our behavior, it is impossible to tell if any internal reality of faith actually exists. Christians, Jews, Muslims, Buddhists, atheists, agnostics and outright pagans will all attempt to adjust their behavior to the established norm.

I should also remark that the changes in a society that either raise or lower this standard happen so slowly that most people are not aware a shift is taking place. It is a truth that can hardly be contested that wherever Christianity has prevailed, it has raised the standard of morals to a place higher than they ever were before. Certain actions that were considered normal among ancient civilizations have now become recognized by every Christian community as deserving severe punishment. In other situations, virtues that were relatively rare have become common. One particular characteristic that Christianity has brought is a more merciful and courteous temper that has softened the uncouth manners and humanized the brutal ferocity that was prevalent in even the most polished of pagan cultures. As previously mentioned, these qualities are produced in a society that has been influenced by Christianity, even among those who do not believe in Christ. Even those who go so far as to reject the claims of Christ will be impacted by the general reformation of the culture. The Temple remained standing in Israel, even though God's glory had departed. I make this observation to point out that when we are inquiring about the true spiritual state of a society, we should not be deceived by superficial appearances.

It may be helpful in determining the advancing or declining state of authentic faith in our country at the present moment, and in determining some of the causes that have led to the current state, to consider how certain conditions in a society tend to impact the state of that culture's faith.

Experience tells us that persecution often has the opposite effect it seeks to produce. As Milton said in *Paradise Lost*, "Her devilish engine recoils back upon herself."[3] Authentic faith has always thrived under persecution. During such times, it is not easy to be a Christian. There are no lukewarm believers or half-hearted followers of Christ in times of great difficulty. The battle lines are clear during such times, and it becomes evident that the kingdom of Christ is not of this world. The greater the difficulty, the closer it drives us to Christ. Only in Him do we find refuge. We truly become pilgrims and strangers. We carefully examine and cling to the basics of the faith. They become an anchor in the storm.

Ironically, peace and prosperity have the opposite effect. When all seems to be going well, we tend to forget that we are engaged in warfare. The intensity of faith that gets us through the tough times tends to languish when life is easy. The Church becomes assimilated into the culture and cultural Christianity replaces authentic faith. The distinctions between Church and culture become blurred.

If this is the case, it is easy to figure out where our country falls at the moment. The Church has become part of the culture. It has blended into the landscape as another institution. It is financially prosperous. It has become a force in politics and the law. Even the clergy are so enmeshed in the concerns of proper society that they have lost their spiritual distinction.

If that is the case with pastors, imagine the impact the continued commercial prosperity of the nation and the progress we have made in all the arts, sciences and all the other marks of an affluent society have had on the maintenance of any *vital* form of Christian faith among the masses. Adam Smith has observed that in an economic situation such as exists in our country at the present time, there tends to be a much looser system of morals in the higher economic groups than in the middle and lower groups in society. Now we see the growth of financial success in the middle classes as a result of their commercial ventures.

When this takes place in a country like ours, with a political system such as we have, wealth also means political influence and power. As wealth trickles down from the wealthy to the lower classes, so do the comforts and refinements of the higher classes, as well as their vices and systems of morality. Add to this the growing urbanization and the opportunities that a great metropolis offers and you can understand some of the roots of the relaxed morality we are presently observing in the culture. We have to admit that even though the commercial spirit has brought great benefits and advancements to our society, it is not by nature a helpful system in terms of maintaining a vital and dynamic faith.

In times like we are living in, ideas of radical obedience and self-denial fade into the background. Even faithful Christians become soft and more tolerant of the moral decline of the world around them. In general, most men and women think little about issues of faith. Since the majority of nominal Christians don't think much about their faith or take the time to study the Bible, it should not surprise us that they are not familiar with the very foundational tenets of authentic Christian faith. Only those principles or doctrines that fit with the general tenor of the culture are observed as common practice. The truths that stand in stark contrast to the systems of the culture are almost totally forgotten. This is especially obvious when these teachings confront the problems of pride, luxury and conformity to the culture. Even the clergy seem afraid to tread too heavily on these subjects in their preaching for fear they will be regarded as fanatics.

When the majority of society drifts this way, we will periodically see some reformer come along who will point these things out. Unfortunately, the way some of these well-intentioned men and women approach these issues is so strange that their efforts are often counterproductive.

It is not as if some will come out and openly deny their Christian faith. That would not be socially acceptable. Some, though, might go so far as to claim the Bible is not anything but a book made up by men, even though those who make such statements are generally ignorant of its contents. When put on the spot, many of these individuals will confess that they do not believe many of the central tenets the Bible teaches.

When you put all these factors together, it becomes clear that when a country has been in a state of spiritual decline for as long as ours has, true faith—already very rare—is in great danger of simply disappearing. Soon, all that will be left is a weak and impotent version of Christianity in which no one talks about their personal faith and religion itself is viewed as the sign of a weak mind. Unbelief itself will become fashionable.

Some might argue that the scenario I have depicted is not an accurate portrayal of the actual condition in our nation. I would have to argue that the true state of faith here does not differ greatly from this picture. Only those who have not taken a careful and objective look at the state of spiritual affairs in this country would deny this conclusion. I will refrain from going into specific examples that support my analysis. Look at the bigger picture and you will see the effects of increasing wealth and luxury, the slow loss of the habits of a more conservative time, and the way relaxed morals have diffused throughout the middle classes.

I am not denying that some good has come with progress. We are a society that enjoys a higher level of refinement and the benefits that come from more common courtesy than the darkness and rudeness of an earlier time. Unfortunately, along with the decline of the darkness, we have also experienced the decline of vital faith. God has been forgotten. He has blessed us with good things, but we are not grateful. He uses life to chastise our moral failures, but we don't heed the warnings. Sunday is no longer a day of worship. It has become a day of pleasure and entertainment. Even when days of national prayer are established, we do not take the few minutes required to attend services. We set business meetings instead. It is an insult to the King of heaven. There is no reflection or repentance. Few traces of authentic faith can be found. As knowledge and information have increased, our understanding of Christianity has diminished. We do not understand its doctrines and we do not live its requirements. Christianity has become a mere system of ethics. Ironically, we do not personally embrace these ethics anyway.

The decline of Christian faith (and all the dimensions of it we have looked at) has at its core one particular cause that I want to address in more detail. There was a time in this land when the Christian faith had all the vitality we have spoken of previously. It was the faith of the multitude of men and women who have made us great.[4] Every page of their writings made the truths of the Christian faith visible, and on these truths they constructed a system of morals beautiful and exalted. If you doubt the influence these men and women had on society, read their works and see how even in our liturgy, the foundations of the faith were strong and vital. If you compare these works with many of the things being written by theologians and clergymen in our time, you will find a great gulf between the two. Some of this tendency, it is true, is a reaction to those men and women who held fast to the basic doctrines of the faith but lived in a way that brought disgrace to the name of Christ.

Toward the end of the last century, the theologians of the institutional Church began to encounter a different error. They began to advocate the objective of promoting the moral and practical dimensions of Christianity, which they believed had been neglected. The problem with their emphasis was not that these things were unimportant but that they stressed these behavioral and external issues without maintaining the importance of the biblical basis for a relationship with Christ. They abandoned teaching the necessity of embracing Christ's atonement as the basis of acceptance with God. They failed to acknowledge that a person's actions as a Christian are rooted in an essential understanding of the foundations of the Christian faith. This was a fatal error. What they were doing was changing the very nature of authentic faith. The result was a watering down of Christian faith that had produced the very virtues they were extolling. They lost the spirit of the faith.

This was an error not easily corrected. As Virgil wrote in the *Aeneid*, "The descent is easy," the implication being that to again ascend is difficult. This faulty approach to true faith has persisted into the present century and, combined with the other problems we have explored, has led to the current state of cultural Christianity. The press has added to the problem by publishing numerous articles on public morality without any attachment or consideration of the basis of faith on which such behavior is motivated. Morality has been divorced from spirituality. Ironically, as the knowledge of the Bible has become more obscure, the moral system itself, divorced from its basis, has begun to whither and die. In these days, not only will you not hear these biblical foundations addressed in the media, but you will also often not hear them addressed in church!

The degree to which the foundations have decayed can be illustrated by the following. When you explore the literature of our day, there is one particular genre of writing that gives a penetrating look at current life and manners. The authors of novels, when they are men and women of astute observation, are able to capture in their work profound insights into human nature. If you make a careful investigation into the most popular of these books that are available, you will find that rarely does faith play a significant role in their content.

It is another indication of how far the spiritual climate has declined. If a minister gives a message that is devoid of biblical content, that minister often still affirms the basics of the faith in their formal liturgy. But in novels, no such vehicle exists. Even in books in which the main characters are Christians and whose lives are portrayed in a positive light, there is no mention of the belief system that has produced such positive characters. You are given the impression that if there were no belief system at all, these characters would act just the same. Such is not the case in books written by those of other faiths such as Islam. Generally speaking, you will find the foundations of their faith articulated clearly in the story. Character is intimately interwoven with belief.

It is also my observation that many of the great writers of our time, unfortunately, are professing unbelievers. Even if a writer is not against religious faith in his or her own writings, it is not uncommon for that writer to praise those who are openly hostile to religious faith. By their endorsement, they reinforce the message these other writers are sending.[5]

Is there any doubt that the handwriting is on the wall for where we are heading? If we look around, we will see the outcome of these trends in countries that are ahead of us in reaching the logical conclusions of such cultural drift. We see in such cases that manners have been corrupted, morality has sunk into depravity, indulgence is out of control and, above all, faith has been discredited and unbelief has become fashionable.[6] When a culture reaches this point, it becomes so out of touch with truth that masses of people deny outright the existence of God. God's will for the nation has been abandoned and man has been made God.

My hunch is that some who acknowledge the decline in religious belief in our nation will claim that I carry my logic to extreme conclusions. They will argue it could never happen here. They also will undoubtedly argue that I am a fanatic and that my view of how culture should be influenced by faith is impractical. They might argue that people who act as I have advocated would be too heavenly minded to be of any earthly good. They would say that if too many were so occupied, the entire machine of civilized society would come to a screeching halt.

In response, I would suggest that such arguments are without merit. At worst, what I have argued that the Bible teaches would call for us to sacrifice a bit of worldly comfort and material affluence for the sake of eternal reward. It is not as if Jesus didn't teach the same thing. He not only suggested we sacrifice when it is required, but He also said we should do it with an attitude of cheerfulness. To respond like this to the call of Christ requires us to hold all temporal possessions loosely. I would agree that were all men and women in our country to follow the challenge of living according to the teachings of Christ, our nation, as it exists, would be unable to function as it does.

Unfortunately, I can assure you that this will never happen in this lifetime. On the other hand, I can also assure you that were such a thing to happen, the entire population would actually be much better off than they are at present. If the entire country followed the law of Christ, we would become a land of peace and prosperity. We would be a place where one could see joy on the face of every citizen.

It is true that in the first century, there were those who interpreted the Christian faith in such a way and left their jobs and families to await the imminent return of Jesus Christ. It didn't take long for the apostle Paul to confront this misuse of the faith. He channeled a proper response to their faith by challenging the believers to tackle their secular activities with more zest and enthusiasm. By doing so, they would bring more honor to Christ.

In light of the current discussion, it is interesting to note that Paul encouraged believers to respond in this way while he also called them to the priority of the love of Christ, an eternal point of view, a healthy indifference to the things of the world and a zeal for growing in spiritual maturity that would lead to the performance of the essential qualities of authentic Christian faith we have been discussing. Obviously, Paul saw no inconsistency between the two. Again, remember that the distinguishing characteristic of authentic faith is *a desire to please God in all our thoughts, and words, and actions; to take the revealed word to be the rule of belief and practice; to "let [our] light so shine before men"* (Matt. 5:16); *and in all things to "adorn the doctrine" we profess* (Titus 2:10).[7]

No occupation is demanded, no pursuit is forbidden, no science or art is prohibited and no pleasure condemned as long as it is consistent with this principle. It must be noted that authentic Christianity does not embrace an inordinate desire or fervor in the pursuit of wealth or fame, nor does it look with favor on politicians who seek office in order to attain admiration, personal power or great affluence instead of serving to seek the peace, comfort and security of the common citizen. Such politicians are power mongers, not public servants. They have forgotten that a nation is the sum of its individuals and that true prosperity is the sum of the total happiness of each individual.

It can also be argued that rather than causing stagnation in relationship to temporal activity, a vital faith can actually provide a proper motivation for the pursuit of social activity that increases a person's effectiveness and enables him or her to better focus his or her energy on the task at hand. It also frees a person from the impact of disappointment when things do not go as planned. It enables the person to trust God for the outcome while working enthusiastically as if the work were his or her service to God. This is, in fact, the "secret" of living a life that is both useful and happy.

The interactions of members of the society are also enhanced when each seeks to live at peace with one another and recognizes the value of all human beings as members of the same family. Any country that was filled with men and women who thought and acted this way would be characterized by a state of harmony seldom, if ever, seen in human history. The discord and petty jealousies that create conflict in most societies would cease to exist, and the culture would run as smoothly as the harmony of the planets in their orbits.

This is what a truly Christian nation would look like. It also would experience a beneficial relationship with other countries with which it interacted. A nation peaceful and happy at home would be respected and loved abroad. The integrity of a truly Christian nation would inspire confidence in its interactions with other nations. Most international disputes find their roots in distrust and jealously. These often lead to more obvious forms of injury. Such things would be minimized by the policies of a Christian nation. And if such a nation were unjustly attacked, the spirit that pervades the nation would provide a powerful dynamic to bring out the greatest resistance to such hostility. Add to all of this the role divine intervention might play on behalf of a nation that sought to serve and honor God in all it does.

Some writers have mistakenly assumed that true faith is an enemy to patriotism. If patriotism is defined in such a way that it is really nationalism—that is, the use of all available power and resources to impose the will of one nation on another—then surely authentic faith is the enemy. But if patriotism is a love for one's country and the desire to see justice, peace and good will toward all men prevail, then faith is not the enemy but the best friend of such patriotism. The opposite theory can only be held by those who have not come to grips with the totality of the teachings of Christ and their implications for the health and strength of a nation. It would be like saying that the principle of gravity is limiting to human freedom without recognizing the role it plays in keeping the universe intact.

It would seem that the best view of patriotism recognizes that society and all its numerous elements are best served when the general welfare of the greatest number of people becomes the great objective of all its people, rather than the selfish pursuit of personal peace and affluence by each individual. A proper response to the call of Christ to love all men, even one's enemies, should produce this outcome in a truly Christian culture. Universal love produces the highest form of patriotism. Benevolence and philanthropy that arise from a purely secular framework usually proves deficient: They always fall short of meeting the full needs of those they seek to benefit. Cost is always measured against the discomfort that such benevolence might produce in the giver. True Christian benevolence goes the extra mile. Its objective is to meet the need even at the cost of self-sacrifice. It is like a river that flows from an unfailing and abundant source. It is like an infection—a good infection—that first influences its immediate surroundings and then begins to spread outward in ever-increasing circles.

You might observe that many of these effects could be produced by any belief system, be it religious or not, that advocated a positive morality and had the ability to enforce its laws. Of course, all such systems must come to grips with the inability of men and women to keep such precepts and the need for a higher power that can assist us in our weakness. In this sense, Christianity has no equal. It not only teaches the highest moral and ethical code known to man, but through relationship with the Creator of the code the believer is empowered by the Holy Spirit to keep it.

True Christianity, by nature, seems to be particularly and powerfully constituted to promote the welfare and health of political communities. Why is that? The reality is that all other systems are rooted in human selfishness. They are conceived in selfishness, grow in selfishness and, ultimately, perish because of selfishness.

This selfishness assumes different forms in different classes of society. Among the upper classes, it can be seen in displays of luxury and the meaningless pursuits and acquisitions that are chased to satisfy vain gratification. Here, where a generous spirit has the ability to produce a great heart, selfishness brings only death. In the lower classes, selfishness finds its expression in prideful insubordination in all its forms. Rich or poor, though the outward forms may vary, the root is the same. Self is put at the center of the person's life and all energy is expended in attempting to fulfill the self's desires and ego-centered aspirations. Thus motivated, such people will be prone to overrate their own merits and accomplishments while underrating those of anyone else. They will tend to overstate the problems in their life while undervaluing those things in life that are to their advantage.

It is these attitudes that create a culture in which people don't care and can't love and in which leaders don't lead and the general population won't follow. Institutions are blamed for life circumstances and personal responsibility does not enter into the equation. Problems are always someone else's fault. Sin and stupidity are never acknowledged, perhaps not even recognized. Where this is the case, there can be no healthy society. The opposite of selfishness is public spirit. Such is the foundation of political health and vitality. It energizes the attitudes and actions that lead to greatness for a nation.

There is certainly an understanding of these factors among the men and women who are the architects of nations and framers of governments. They seek to inspire the one while repressing the other. Sometimes leaders have gone to extremes in these attempts. Ancient Sparta flourished for more than 700 years under a system that discouraged selfishness by prohibiting commerce and imposing poverty and hardship on her citizens. The same could be said of the Roman Empire. Public spirit was the equivalent of the love of glory, both for the empire and for its heroes. The result was an insatiable hunger for conquest that eventually led to Rome's downfall. When public vitality depends on conquest, vitality languishes when conquest is gone. Wealth and luxury produce stagnation, and stagnation terminates in death.

When the continuance of the state can only be purchased at the suffering and poverty of its citizens, the means has sacrificed the ends to achieve its own purposes. This is self-defeating. Men and women unite in a civilized society to attempt to achieve the greatest happiness for the greatest number. There was not much happiness among the common people of Sparta or any other society so constituted. Nor can a society long survive whose basis of existence is the misery of other cultures. It, like Rome, becomes the enemy of its neighbors and the scourge of the human race. All these outcomes are examples of what happens when man attempts to be God. All efforts turn out to have faults in their execution and fail to achieve their purposes.

This leads me to comment on the greatness of the constitution under which we live in this country. I would argue that of all governments that have ever existed, ours has excelled at balancing both the motivation to accomplish a degree of public spirit while maintaining the individual's ability to achieve a life of quietness, comfort and goodness. Our system is structured in such a way that selfishness has no advantage. My objective is not, however, to praise our political system but to show how Christianity is in every way opposed to the very enemy of political communities: selfishness.

We could say that the primary purpose of true Christianity is to root out natural selfishness and all that comes with it in order to help us develop a proper sense of who we are and what our obligations are to our fellow human beings. Benevolence is the driving principle of authentic Christianity. It is a direct result of developing a lifestyle of moderation in the pursuit of pleasure and affluence, a degree of indifference to the things culture has decided are important, diligence in the performance of personal and civil responsibilities, a commitment to doing the will of God, and a patient and trusting attitude toward the providence of God in one's response to the unpredictable and often discouraging events of life. A life of authentic faith will produce humility in our lives. Humility is essential if a man or woman is to develop a spirit of genuine benevolence.

In whatever sector of society Christian faith exists, it sets out to fight against the cost to human dignity that selfishness has exacted. It teaches the wealthy to be generous and to have a proper view of the privileges and responsibilities that come with financial success. When wealth is used properly and those who have it demonstrate humility, the inequalities of life are less bitter to those who do not possess it. On the other hand, for those who live in less-affluent circumstances, authentic faith teaches diligence, patience, industry and a recognition that the faithful execution of their responsibilities is to be done without envy of the rich or bitterness toward their own state.

Contentment is a product of recognizing that the way things are is not the way that they should be and that one day they will be as God intended. The amount of energy put into the pursuit of worldly wealth, power and fame is not worth the ultimate value of the pursuit. The great benefit of authentic faith is that it produces a state of inner peace that gives much greater satisfaction than the most expensive pleasure can provide. It is not limited by any social, economic or racial barrier. In some ways, it is a benefit not to have to deal with the variety of temptations that wealth affords. There is much to be said for a simple life. The true treasure for people of faith is the inheritance that Christ now keeps for them that will one day be theirs.

It is important to note that the requirement for all these benefits to occur is a real, deep, authentic faith. Nominal or superficial Christianity does not have the ability to create such outcomes. Political decay can thrive under cultural Christianity, but authentic faith will bring it to a sudden halt. As things stand at the present moment, we need authentic faith desperately. If we do not pursue such faith as a nation, not only will we not experience the great benefits that such faith brings, but we will also be in danger of losing the blessings we enjoy as a result of such faith in the past. We are headed toward a society that incurs the multitude of evils that result from living with no religion at all.

A nominal faith might survive and have some small benefit when the society in which it exists favors its continuance. But when a culture has deteriorated to the condition ours has, it will take a vital faith for Christianity to survive at all. In times past, we enjoyed a society in which faith was not only practiced but also honored. Much has changed. Not only have we ceased to practice the faith of our forefathers, but we also now look at that faith as if it were some strange aberration of a time gladly gone. Respect for the past has ceased to exist. The danger now exists of the collapse of a system due to the lack of belief in the principles on which it was based.

We have reached a point in which a serious infusion of the authentic faith that was the life force of our religious institutions is necessary in order for those institutions to survive. The Church today is run by men and women who are so different from and who hold such different beliefs from those who founded these institutions that the Church's very survival is threatened. The degree to which an authentic and vital faith can be re-infused into our churches will be the degree to which these institutions will be reformed and once again become vital.

We live in a state of cultural decline. A dry, unanimated religiosity does not have the ability to inspire the masses. Anyone who thinks otherwise knows little of human nature. People are looking for reality and authenticity in spiritual matters. Even if the upper classes are content to go through the religious motions, the common man will not tolerate such a charade. Philosophy might be adequate for the rich, but the man or woman on the street needs a faith that is real and works in his or her life. Experience tells us that the common person is not looking for complicated theology. Theology is irrelevant to these individuals. But the kind of vital faith of which I speak knows no social boundaries. It is more likely to be embraced by the common person than by the upper classes that are held more in bondage to the materialistic spirit of the age. Everywhere vital faith invades, we will see people and societies transformed from barbarism to a state of sobriety, decency, industry and whatever else makes men and women productive members of society.

If, by God's grace, a new wave of true spirituality were to break forth and gain ground, there is no way of predicting the way public morals and the political welfare of the nation would benefit. The encroachment of toxic decay would be forced to cease. The blessings of God would once again be released in our land.

The result of such not happening is almost too horrid to think about. What would happen were faith to vanish from our nation? This should be the question every prudent individual should ponder. The Church as we know it, with all its flaws and inconsistencies, would cease to exist. How can anyone think such an outcome would be anything other than disastrous for society? What impact would this have on the moral fiber of the common person? The restraint against moral deviation would be greatly lowered. Where would people who desire to change their lives and live in relationship with God and according to His teachings go? Who would be examples of the kind of lives we should live? What would become of the heritage handed down by the Church through the centuries? How would we avoid creating a degenerate posterity? To what depth might public morality sink? It is probably good that such a society could not last for long. When the cement that has held a nation together no longer exists, the state soon dissolves into anarchy.

Let me also point out that nothing inherent in the advanced nature of our society will be able to stop the degeneracy that threatens us. History teaches that many of the most advanced civilizations the world has known were also societies that contained the most shocking degree of moral decay. The same can be said for some of our modern neighbors. Although they appear polished and refined on the outside, the state of moral toxicity of their societies is alarming.

What can account for this corruption? The apostle Paul made the observation that the Roman Empire had sunk into the mire of moral depravity because it had rejected the knowledge of God (see Rom. 1:28). Let this serve as a warning. It would be a tragic mistake to think that even though the moral fiber of our country has deteriorated, our prosperity and wealth will keep us from drifting further. Nor let us imagine that the fate of Rome might never be our own. If God gave up on us, our fate would surely be the same. And what would keep God from doing so? We actually might be in a worse spot than those in these ancient civilizations. Their only restraint was based on human philosophy and natural conscience. We, on the other hand, have the advantage of having the Bible, as well as the knowledge of how God dealt with them, to direct our path. The logic of the situation would indicate that if God allowed their nations to sink to the logical consequences of their depravity, would He not also do the same with us, with the same result?

What shall we do? This is the critical question we all should be asking. The answer is not complicated. The cause of the decline of faith and the decay of morals are the arrows that point to what would be expedient for us to pursue with the greatest degree of urgency. The problems we face as a society should be viewed as spiritual problems rather than merely political issues. This is a perspective that does not even appear to be considered by the media. What can we expect from the kinds of solutions they offer? Certainly they would only produce transient progress, not fundamental change. What needs to happen is that every effort must be made to raise the standards of public morality in our nation. This is a responsibility that falls especially on people who have influence and power, whether political or financial.

Not only should people in these positions exercise their authority and abilities to this end, but also they themselves should serve as the best examples of what this means by striving for the highest spiritual and moral progress in their own lives. It is important to become involved with those of power and influence who are responsible for the decline of which we have been speaking. Some will be called to attempt to influence the system from within. Let me caution you. This is a calling with particular challenges. You must be careful how much of the system you embrace to accomplish this task. Sometimes, the Christian in this setting becomes indistinguishable from the unbeliever. To accomplish this balance takes all the discipline and fortitude you can muster. Remember, the time has come to draw a line in the sand and decide on which side you will take your stand.[8] It is from this commitment that the real adventure begins.

There are reasons why I take this position. One is the observation that when a great task needs to be undertaken, men and women will tend to rise to the level of challenge the task requires. They are not prone to give heroic effort to an undertaking that is regarded as easy or matter-of-fact. When there is great adventure and challenge involved, they are willing to pay the price. Men and women will endure hardship and difficulty and give it all they have when the task is viewed as heroic. When the action required is not as exciting and demanding, they will tend to approach it with less than full effort and might fail to achieve the goal for that very reason. In the circumstances we face, change will require wholehearted devotion to the cause. Such devotion requires a clear delineation between those who promote a vital faith and those who oppose anything that is too "Christian." If you are of such a character that you want the best for your country, the time to hesitate is past. It is time to count the cost and decide what needs to be done to enable you to be the most effective person you can be in the renewal of the moral and spiritual life of the nation. The one who takes this attitude is the true patriot.

It is not only necessary that people of influence and authority set an example in this area, as important as that may be, but they also need to encourage others to do the same. They should get involved in any efforts that are launched to promote the progress of moral and spiritual renewal. Above all these efforts, there must be a focused effort to teach these values to the next generation. Our children are going to have to deal with the outcome of our neglect of these critical values. They will be under siege by the ideas and examples of those who have no place in their lives for true faith.

It feels as if we live in a world in which a brood of moral vipers has been hatched that are waiting to unleash themselves on the world. But let me make myself clear: All attempts to restore or protect the values and morals that have made this nation great will be in vain without the restoration of a vital *Evangelical*

Christianity.[9] Without this firm foundation it will be impossible to elevate the state of values in the future. Valiant and perhaps momentarily successful efforts will eventually fail, and society will sink back to the levels of morality that previously existed. This is why it is so essential that we exercise all our efforts to revive the vital faith our forefathers possessed.

If the Church is to experience this renewal, change needs to begin with the ministers of these local churches. Their convictions will determine the health of the various congregations. Wherever men and women have faithfully taught the Bible, their efforts have been greatly rewarded. It probably doesn't need to be said, but generally speaking, these men and women are also friends of the civil authorities whom they attempt to support. For those who fear that spiritual renewal will lead to occasional disorderly and irregular exhibitions, which are to the detriment of the institution, they should know that such disturbances are not the norm. It is in fact the duty of all who serve in the clergy to seek to promote a vital faith in the Church. Some are already engaged in such work.

Our schools and universities must also encourage the study of those classics that promoted morality and vital spirituality. In the past, such works were at the core of a university education. Now, they are wholly ignored. Things have gotten so far out of hand in our time that not even theological seminaries require the reading of these works. The result is a form of preaching in many of our churches that is devoid of authentic spiritual content.

I solemnly submit these ideas to all who have at heart the welfare of the nation. It is time to take action. It might be necessary to come to grips with whether such action is properly motivated or merely an attempt to gain some kind of personal power or political advantage. It also might be necessary to unjustly endure the false claims of opponents who accuse us of such. But because it is God's pleasure to design things in such a way that authentic faith and pure morality enhance the welfare of the state and the preservation of an orderly society, it would seem foolish to oppose such action on the grounds that someone's motives might not be pure.

Oh, that God might help us take to heart the pursuit of the kind of life this text has suggested! How great it would be to experience the outcome for our nation and our families if we lived like this! How great to live in a land where men and women possessed authentic faith and not a cultural counterfeit of it! We would experience that which the poet Horace prayed for:

> Restore your light, O excellent chief
> To your country; for it is like spring
> Where your countenance has appeared;
> To the people the day passes more pleasantly,
> And the sun shines more brightly.[10]

Notes

1. Wilberforce is referring to England in 1797.
2. Wilberforce made this observation in Parliament on a number of occasions, quoting intellectuals as anti-religious as Machiavelli.
3. John Milton, *Paradise Lost*, bk. 4, lines 17-18.
4. Wilberforce here lists a large number of bishops and archbishops of the Anglican Church in the sixteenth and seventeenth centuries. The list also includes one theologian and one Presbyterian minister.

5. Wilberforce's notes on this passage refer to Dr. William Robertson's low view of the Mosaic authorship of the Pentateuch and the same man's praise of Gibbon's *Rise and Fall of the Roman Empire,* published during this period. In the notes to another edition of this book, Wilberforce also remarks on the comments of a minister in support of the works of David Hume, a professing unbeliever and famous philosopher of the time.

6. Wilberforce is again alluding to the state of affairs in France.

7. The italics are from Wilberforce.

8. It should be noted that this was Wilberforce's own approach. He worked from within the political system to bring change. He also formed societies made up of some of the wealthiest men and women in England to tackle the social issues of his time. It was said that he made goodness fashionable!

9. Wilberforce's exact expression and italicized emphasis.

10. Horace, *Odes,* bk. 4, 5, 5.

PRACTICAL HINTS ABOUT AUTHENTIC FAITH

Section One: *Faith That Is Not Faith*[1]

U p to this point in the book, I have attempted to paint a picture of the problems with the cultural Christianity that plagues this nation. I have pointed out the low view of Christian faith held in general, the faulty ideas held concerning virtually every major doctrine of the faith, and the result of lowering the standard set for the behavior of true believers by settling for a cultural substitute. I hope I have also shown how most people totally miss the incredible power and beauty of true biblically based Christian faith. The totality of the package is so ingenious that is bears the mark of its divine origin.

As we approach the end of this exploration, I would ask you to be careful not to think that there is no great difference between authentic faith and cultural Christianity. The difference between the two is not simply a matter of different opinions but lies at the very heart of the religious debate in our country. The difference between the two is so critical that I will be bold enough to declare: *Their Christianity is not Christianity.*[2] It is false at its core. It lacks the very basic elements that make

Christianity the faith taught by Jesus. I would ask you to pray that those who have been ensnared by this charade would take a close look at the Bible and compare what they believe and how they act with what the Bible clearly teaches. I am hopeful that they will recognize the shallow substitute for which they have settled.

If you happen to fall into this category and are inclined to take a look at your own faith, let me warn you: Most of us have a natural inclination to practice self-inquiry with a predisposition to think better of ourselves than the facts warrant. In other words, most of us are self-deceived in these matters. Selfishness is the root problem. Selfishness will always avoid acknowledging the truth that we are selfish. Our egos defend themselves from such honest scrutiny. The result is that we tend to overrate our positive qualities and overlook our negative qualities. So be careful when you evaluate yourself. Always take into consideration the nature of the selfish ego and remember that it does not have the ability to clearly evaluate its own morality.

We need to see our true state as God sees it. Because of His perfect purity and His ability to know us better than we know ourselves, it is likely that He sees problems and failures we are barely conscious of—if we recognize them at all. God always operates in the now. Over time, our defense systems have the ability to dull the conviction of the acts and attitudes that violate God's holiness. Remorse can turn to faint recognition. But God still knows those actions in the now. Think of the implications of this observation for the person who has not had an authentic encounter with Jesus Christ or embraced His finished work on the cross as the payment for all sin. What if this person had to appear before Christ at this very moment with the full impact and offensive nature of every sin he or she has ever committed revealed in His presence? When I imagine such a scene, it helps me come to grips with the true state of my spiritual life. It is always sobering.

This might be a good time to point out some other common sources of self-deception. Many of us are reinforced in our over blown estimates of ourselves due to the praise we receive from other people. In the realm of faith, we are often deceived into thinking that if we know and believe the right things, we are all right with God. We forget that God is looking for a faith that not only believes intellectually but also has a heartfelt passion for those truths and enough true faith to put them into action.

There is another source of deception that I feel the need to point out. It seems that there are certain vices that afflict us and certain virtues that are more natural at different seasons of our life. If we are going to have an accurate assessment of ourselves, we need to focus on that area of our life in which we are the most susceptible. The writer of Hebrews refers to this as "the sin that so easily entangles" (Heb. 12:1). In the same way, we ought to be careful when we use some strength or virtue that comes naturally to our disposition as a guide to our true state. We need to evaluate those areas of our life that are more likely to reveal our true nature. We tend to judge ourselves in exactly the opposite way, focusing on our strengths and avoiding our weaknesses. The result of this kind of evaluation is to let ourselves settle for less than God requires of us.

A more subtle form of self-deception occurs when we move out of a period of life in which some form of sin has had a stranglehold on us. If at a later time we no longer have the problem,

we might mistakenly think that it is the change in our character that accomplished the task of reformation. What has probably actually happened is that some new form of temptation
has taken the place of the old. The new temptation, in all like-
lihood, is simply more suited to our new stage of life. No true
transformation has taken place.

Let's take a closer look at this. At one point in life, boys tend
to be overwhelmed with their sexual desire for girls. Girls, on the
other hand, tend to be guilty of excessive vanity and the pursuit
of other forms of pleasure. If the children are not openly rebel-
lious or always causing trouble, the males might be thought of
as *good-hearted* young men and the females as *innocent* young
women.[3] The parents of these young men and women might
have little interest in the state of their children's spiritual lives.
In fact, the parents might assume that even though their children have little interest in religion at this point in their lives,
they will surely become more interested as they grow older. It is
totally outside the parents' frame of reference to think of such
young people as living outside the favor of God, destitute of any
spiritual virtue and in a disastrous and dangerous position as
they face the future.

The children grow older and get married. For the boy, the
former attitude toward sex that he exhibited is not considered
appropriate for a married man. His earlier actions are viewed as
"sowing his wild oats." Now he is required to be a person of
solid character. In the same way, if the young woman is still too
consumed with her own appearance or other issues of vanity
after marriage, she will not be found to be acting appropriately. Yet if they meet the expectations of family and society, they

will probably be known as good people. The fact that they might be in a disastrous spiritual condition is still not understood. Their life situations have changed and their outward behavior has adjusted, but they are no closer to living in a right relationship with God than they were before marriage. They might feel good about themselves and think they are living good lives, but in all probability whatever kind of life they are living is still dominated by the principle of self-interest. Even their reform from previous vices is motivated by the desire to avoid any behavior that might negatively influence their success in society.

Let's fast-forward to old age. You might think that with the coming of age the same young man and woman would finally begin to take eternal things more seriously. But such is not the case. They have maintained proper behavior so that they might be socially acceptable. Now the expectation is that they will be good natured and cheerful, as all elderly men and women should be. They are expected to cultivate a certain tolerance for the actions of the young, remembering that they themselves were young once also.

This is the exact opposite of what should be happening. When men or women come into a state of authentic faith, they should look back on the actions of their pre-Christian days with a sense of shame and sorrow. Rather than tolerate or condone the actions of the young that are clearly outside God's will, they should warn the young of how the same behavior in their youth caused them nothing but regret. However, instead of seeing these kinds of wise older men and women, we see men and women who have lived in a state of self-deception for so many years that they have no such wisdom to offer the young. In every stage of life, they have devised schemes to keep themselves from dealing with the true state of their hearts and their desperate need for Jesus Christ. Conviction has been replaced by complacency.

I know that some people are going to think I'm being fanatical when I suggest these things. I personally think the time to worry about social or political correctness has run its course. Look at the dangerous state we are in. Those who might find these observations to be fanatical have no spiritual concern for actual people. Their talk is all rhetoric. How are the ones who think this way going to feel when the end of time comes? What will they think when they realize they have been misguided and are culpable for the shattered lives of their children and loved ones? What about those who should know better but are more concerned with what people think than with what God has said?

There is a great deal of talk about the need for love. Most of it is just talk. True love has at its heart the welfare of the ones who are loved. It carefully studies the circumstances of its beloved to make sure nothing will be of harm to them. When true love senses danger, it seeks to protect, regardless of the social consequences. This is the love of a parent for a dear child or a wife or husband toward a spouse for whom he or she deeply cares. We applaud the efforts of mothers and fathers who carefully tend to the physical needs of their children. But what about tending to their spiritual needs? True love cares about eternal welfare. Anything else is merely some form of indifference, regardless of what it is called. It lulls itself into a state of blissful denial.

If you are careful and considerate, you will be alarmed that so many parents take for granted the formative years when young children can be influenced and shaped. They seem to think that if their children are cheerful and appear to be happy, they have done their job. This is the very time when, in a spirit of happiness and joy, the important lessons about life and God can be taught. This is the time when habits can be formed that will help young men and women resist the inevitable temptations that will come their way as they grow older.

I might be accused of being sexist, but this is especially true of young women, who seem by nature to have greater sensitivity to spiritual things than young men. It is as if God has equipped women in a special way to undertake the spiritual formation of young children. It will seem old fashioned I'm sure, but it seems to me that this quality in women makes them doubly valuable as marriage partners. A wife is especially equipped to be an instrument of divine care to her husband when he returns from the battle of his daily labor. Her tenderness can bring healing to the wounds suffered throughout the day.

It is quite something when you think about a man and woman, committed to each other in marriage, coming before God in a spirit of gratitude and praying for His care in their lives and the life of their family. They are able to trust in God's goodness and provision when life delivers uncertainties. They can live with the confidence that whatever may come, God is at work for the good of those who love and trust Him (see Rom. 8:28). They know that one day this life will end and that they will share forever the things God has prepared for those who love Him. This is a great responsibility—to be the instrument of divine formation—and when a woman takes on this task, it is no small affair. Those who tackle this role will have great influence, not only in the present, but also for generations to come.

Unfortunately, this is not the role most women in our society have assumed. Instead of being the instrument of divine instruction, they have taken all the measures they can to ensure that their daughters are brought up to succeed in the ways of the current culture. Instead of nurturing a devotional spirit in them, they promote the love of pleasure and the pursuit of personal vanity.

Innocent young women! Good-hearted young men! Where is the *innocence?* What passes for *goodness of heart?*[4] Remember, we are fallen beings, born in sin, and by nature depraved. Christian faith does not begin with the premise of innocence or goodness of heart. That is optimistic humanism, not authentic faith. Christianity proclaims the need for forgiveness and transformation. We are not what we were meant to be.

Do we see in young men and women today the characteristics that the Bible teaches are outward signs of being in right relationship with God? Or do we see what would appear to be the exact opposite? Do our youth not exhibit behavior that indicates they are alienated from God? Do they love God with all their heart, mind, soul and strength (see Luke 10:27)? Are they seeking first the kingdom of God and His righteousness (see Matt. 6:33)? Don't we really see that they are completely self-centered and self-indulgent? They seem to be "lovers of pleasure" rather than lovers of God (2 Tim. 3:4).

Is church a place to which they go with excitement and expectation, or with dread? It would appear that most of the time, they go to church with reluctance, participate only because they have been forced to do so, and quit going altogether as soon as they are old enough to rebel against their parents. They love to have parties but have no idea what it means to worship. Young men live to have sex with young women and are consumed by the thought. Young women are consumed with vanity and find their chief happiness in shopping and conforming to the latest fads. They love shops, not church.

When these young men and women become adults, they get married, have children and become respectable. But do we see the true transformation of character of which the Bible speaks? The Bible is filled with statements about the necessity of experiencing a new spiritual birth and a transformation of character in which the old nature is the enemy and the new nature is in a life and death conflict with it. God is after true righteousness and holiness. The outward manifestations of this change will be all the things I have previously pointed out. These men and women will be sober, self-controlled, overcome the temptations that previously ruled their lives and will give their energies to the pursuit of things that really matter. But all these will simply be the outward expressions of an inner reality. Without this essential inner change, these young men and women will fall into the routine that Horace so eloquently describes:

> With altered aims, the age and spirit of the man
> Seeks wealth and friends, becomes a slave to ambition,
> And is fearful of having done what it will soon
> Be eager to change.[5]

This is a point of infinite importance; so let me emphasize it one more time by looking at it from another angle. Think of this life as a kind of military camp in which you receive basic training for eternity. You are on probation until the final test, and your job is to pass the test by resisting those things that previously consumed you. When you are young, this means you need to take a stand against immorality and impurity and seek to be thoughtful and industrious. When you get older, the challenges change. You aren't as tempted by the things that tempted you when you were not married or didn't have a family. Now you are tempted to be consumed by the cares of life and concerns for your family. You are faced with ambition and your drive for wealth.

These are the things that keep you from having a proper sense of priority for the things of God. You will be tempted to settle for cultural Christianity and will not be willing to pay the price for the real thing. The former fits your ambition better. Your faith will not really be authentic faith at all. You will remain ignorant of the basic truths of the Bible. You will think of yourself as a Christian because everyone who lives in this country is a Christian. You will bear no signs of transformation, either in your thinking or behavior. Jesus has a message for you. It is found in the book of Revelation: "Wake up! Strengthen what remains and is about to die, for I have not found your deeds complete in the sight of my God" (Rev. 3:2).

If you are willing to listen to this warning and not settle for a cultural Christianity but desire to know and possess authentic faith, it is time for you to step away from the crowd. God is at work in your life. Get away to a place where no one is around and get down on your knees and pray. Ask God to take away your spiritual indifference and insensitivity and enable you to draw close to Him. Ask Him to take away the false thinking that has blinded you and enable you to see and know the truth. Get honest with God. Tell Him you know your true condition or, at least, the lie you have been living. Tell Him, "I have sinned against You." Turn to Him. Tell Him you are sorry. Tell Him you want to change. Tell Him you want to be His man or woman. Think about Jesus and what He did on the cross for you. Thank Him that He died for you. Open your inner being to God and ask Christ to come into your life and live in and through you. Ask the Holy Spirit to begin to work in you from the inside out, to make you the man or woman God designed you to be. Ask God to help you know His will and give you the strength to do it.

Spend some time thinking about the fact that God loves you. Contemplate that all Jesus did, He did for you, as an expression of that love. Reflect on the fact that God has a plan for your life that He wants to reveal to you. It will be the best life you could ever live. Tell Him you want to do what He wants you to do.

Embrace grace. It is a gift for you. It cost Jesus His life. He suffered to make it all possible. It is a gift you haven't earned. It was not given to you because you were "good" but because God loves you. When you really grasp this, you will surrender yourself into His hands. Nothing else makes any sense. You will resolve that by that grace, you will from here forward give all that you are to His service.

So what is your job? According to Paul, it is to "work out your salvation with fear and trembling," relying on the enabling power of the One "who works in you to will and to act according to his good purpose" (Phil. 2:12-13). You are to work out what He has worked in, with a reliance on God's help that is based on your understanding of your weakness and His strength. When you set your mind to do this, He will be there to protect you and keep you secure in Him. It is as if you have enlisted in the military and now live under His insignia. God will be faithful and accomplish His purposes in your life right up to the very end.

When this becomes your set purpose, you have taken on a great task. To stay the course in a world like ours and a culture like ours, you have to decide that you will take all human opinion for exactly what it is worth. You will not hold it higher than it deserves, nor be afraid when it turns against you and attempts to discourage you from your commitment. When you face opposition, attempt to picture in your mind that great host of men and women who have gone before you and kept the faith. You must cultivate this healthy indifference to the opinions and favor of men and women who are not walking with Christ. You can't walk the fence. Such a balancing act will always lead to conflict as you try to please God and the world around you. You won't please either one and you will become miserable. Instead, consistently remember your own flaws and areas of weakness. If you truly "hunger and thirst for righteousness" (Matt. 5:6), you will find this to be a challenge that always reminds you of your weakness and of Christ's mercy and grace.

This is a paradox that the men and women of the world cannot understand: As we grow in Christian maturity, we will also grow in humility. This is the primary principle on which vital faith rests. To the degree that humility grows, so grows our vitality. To the degree it diminishes, our vitality will also diminish. From beginning to end, authentic faith is based on humility.

It takes humility to acknowledge our true state before God and throw ourselves on His mercy. It takes humility to recognize that nothing we can do can change the true state of our heart; only surrender to Christ and opening our heart to the Holy Spirit can enable us to change at all. How we relate to God, to ourselves and to our fellow men and women is all a function of the humility we possess.

The practical benefits of this kind of humility are too numerous to address here. Some are obvious. Humility will keep us from sin. You will view sin as a deadly disease you wish to avoid at all costs. Humility will be your guide and teach you how to interact with the culture in which you live. You will make all decisions based on your passionate desire not to grieve the Spirit of God (see Eph. 4:30). When your heart wants to please God in all things, the very mundane tasks of daily living become acts of worship. You don't become religious; you become authentic. This is the attitude that becomes the purifying agent that changes everything. You then can trust God to lead you and show you what you need to do to serve Him. You become sensitive to His leading.

To keep in this frame of mind, it is essential that you keep your mind on Christ. Prayer will become like breathing for you. Conscience will become sensitive to your faulty desires. Seek to be useful. Avoid idleness. Never settle for what you have already accomplished. Keep striving to be and do all you can. Run the race that has been set before you (see Heb. 12:1-2).

We will be able to measure how we are doing by keeping track of how we love God and our fellow human beings. This is the principle on which all our activity rests. We experience a little bit of heaven when we live according to it. To live according to this rule is to reflect something of the image of God being renewed within us. All is done in love.

Cultural Christians do not understand this. They view service to God as something to be avoided or, at best, endured. They think it must be some boring and negative exercise. They don't know what they are missing. They always ask the wrong questions. They want to know how little they have to give. They want to know how close to the line they can get. They don't want their actions to be challenged. In other words, they only know a negative substitute for authentic faith. For them, Christianity is nothing but a set of rules telling them what they can't do. True faith, with all its beauty and joy, is beyond their comprehension. The only faith they know is not fit for life in the world but only in the monastery.

True Christians have an entirely different outlook on their faith. It is a joy for them to serve the Lord. They don't live lives of obedience out of some heartless obligation to a punitive deity. They live joyfully in the blessing of the life God designed. They aren't looking for a boundary line to push to the limits. They are far away, seeking to get as close as possible to Christ. They seek out like-minded friends with whom they can make this journey together. Such a band of friends reinforces the work of God in each other's lives and motivates each to care for the other. There is no indifference here, as it would be the first sign of spiritual decline. They look forward to times of devotion and worship. Such times infuse their faith with renewed vigor. This kind of faith is filled with happiness.

Men and women who possess authentic faith know that this world is not their final destiny. In a sense, they are just passing through. They are pilgrims and strangers who fight the forces of darkness and temptation that encroach upon them at every turn. They wage war against that part of their own nature that resists the will of God. The struggle of the journey itself inspires a desire to live in that place and time when all corruption, decay and bondage will have passed away. Looking forward to being with Christ forever, true Christians overcome the fear of death. They look forward to what lies beyond. Their attitude is that of Cicero's:

O greatest of days, when I shall hasten to that divine
Assembly and gathering of souls, and when I shall
Depart from this crowd and rabble of life![6]

Some people may suggest that a vigorous faith denies a man or woman the innocent amusements and pleasures of normal life, but this is a myth that the experience of the true believer debunks. Only those whose own experience is nominal at best hold this gloomy view of authentic faith. Let me comment on this fallacy.

First of all, authentic faith does not prohibit any type of amusement or entertainment that is *really* innocent. But who is to decide what is innocent? Cultural Christianity might endorse entertainment that is only consistent with a cultural view of morality and far less demanding than the morality of the Bible. The question that needs to be asked is whether the recreation is in fact recreation and if the entertainment will enhance our relationship with God. The very word "recreation" implies activity that refreshes our bodies, restores our mental energies and renews our spiritual vitality. How much of what is called recreation in our culture has this effect? Whatever fatigues either the body or the mind instead of refreshing them is not really recreation. Whatever entertainment consumes more time, money or energy than is expedient or necessary is not entertaining to the person who knows the true value of these commodities. Certainly any recreation or entertainment that is enjoyed at the cost of the welfare of another human being is not appropriate for the person who lives to share the love of Christ.

So, do Christians never relax or have fun? Certainly they do. God has provided a multitude of ways to provide good, proper recreation and amusement. The Christian just seeks to avoid those activities that are questionable. It is amazing that God created us so that every faculty we have been endowed with to accomplish His purposes is also designed to be an instrument that gives us pleasure. God has designed us in such a way that even the uncertainties of life can be a source of the enjoyment that comes from a simple change of pace. At times, just a variation in the tasks we are working to accomplish is better recreation than some unproductive and unfruitful form of entertainment.

Even so, there are still many different kinds of innocent relaxation. Imagination, taste, genius, nature and art are all at our disposal. True Christians find relaxation in the company of friends and the interaction of social intercourse. They enjoy the benefits of the experience of love, hope, confidence, joy and all other sources of good will extended toward others. In the exercise of these qualities, the giver often receives more than the one to whom he or she gives. I feel sorry for those who have never experienced the delight such a lifestyle brings and who instead must rely on frivolous experiences or sensual gratification to entertain themselves!

The true tragedy occurs when men and women who know only this distorted form of cultural Christianity attempt to give up the pleasures of the world but have no true spiritual experience to meet this need. They have no experience of the love and joy of Christ in their lives. For them, this form of self-denial is like cultural torture. They become hopelessly religious and can't enjoy either the passing pleasures of social amusement or the superior experience of true Christian joy. You can usually recognize them by their dour appearance and the lack of any sense of joy on their faces.

It is true that when a man or woman of true faith has lived a life of unrestrained license, comes to faith in Christ and then begins the process of allowing his or her life to be transformed, many difficulties may be experienced. Old habits die hard, even when the Spirit is at work. Often, these appetites can be accompanied by a sense of guilt for a life poorly lived, especially when the full implications of the atonement of Christ have not yet been realized or applied to his or her life. It is rare that such a state of unrest lasts for long. God has a way of breaking though. He instills a sense of the hope of future progress in the heart of the repentant believer. He seems to have a special affection for those who come to Him with "a broken and contrite heart" (Ps. 51:17).

I don't want you to think that when I speak of the good things that come with true faith that there is not a struggle involved. The truth is that when we live a committed life for Christ, we will have a degree of struggle that will require discipline and tough obedience till the end. Remember, we are at war.

We battle a culture that is out of tune with God, a personality shaped outside the influence of the Holy Spirit, and an unseen universe in which powerful evil forces are allowed to exercise a degree of autonomy until Jesus Christ returns. But along with the battles come times of great joy and deep satisfaction.

This way of life requires that we go all the way in our faith. A shallow faith, even if based on the truth, will not be adequate to complete the journey. One will either go deeper or drift backward. The call to the believer is constant: "Further up and further in!"[7] Without such vigilance, you might end up with just enough faith to make you miserable on your way to heaven. A little faith can make you gloomy. A little faith will not be adequate to lead you into the freedom of obedience, but it will make what once was the pleasure of sin a miserable experience. When someone tells of the joy of following Christ, you will joylessly respond, "I tried it but it didn't work." The truth is, in all probability, you never really tried it. Faith is not something you try. It is a reality you cast yourself upon without reserve.

Some of the pleasure of being a Christian is obvious even to nonreligious people. They might be willing to acknowledge that committed Christians can actually have some fun and excitement in life, but they have no way of understanding the deeper source of happiness in the life of authentic faith. How can they know how it feels to live with the quiet humility of knowing that you have been reconciled to God? How can they process the thought that you are now an object of God's favor and that He cares for you? The peace of mind that comes from this kind of a relationship with Christ is beyond cultural Christians' ability to comprehend. What in their experience would ever enable them to know the peace that comes from the confidence that God is all-wise, all-knowing and all-powerful, and that He has committed Himself to your welfare, both now and forever? How could they ever know how it feels to have confidence that whatever life brings, ultimately God is going to cause all things to work together for your good (see Rom. 8:28)?

When you are young and vigorous and everything seems to be going your way, you might not have the sense of need for authentic faith. But when things go bad—when business fails, those you thought were friends forsake you, or your health begins to fail— then the benefits of a life of faith begin to show their infinite superiority over everything else people settle for instead of Christ. There is almost no more tragic sight than an older man or woman who has missed the only source of true satisfaction. How disturbing to see them still attempting to pursue the pleasures of their youth that are now beyond their grasp. The final season of life is bitter for such people. All is gloom and misery. They look back with vain longing and forward without hope.

Compare this to the final days of true Christians. When their strength fades and their abilities decline, they can look forward without fear and with confidence that the best is yet to come. They can knock on death's door with the expectation that Someone is waiting and has prepared for their coming. Their focus is not on an inheritance left behind but on one waiting to be claimed. They trust in the words of the apostle Paul: "No eye has seen, no ear has heard, no mind has conceived what God has prepared for those who love him" (1 Cor. 2:9). Find men and women who have reached this point after living lives of authentic faith and see what God has done in their lives.

We have never lived in a time when it was more important to seek happiness beyond the sources the world has to offer. We have witnessed the fleeting nature of all earthly possessions. Wealth, power and prosperity are all transitory and uncertain. But true faith lasts, and God always delivers. Even in adversity, faith comes through. Even the true believer rarely experiences the tremendous riches of authentic faith in times of prosperity and peace. But when all these are swept away by the rude hand of time or the rough blast of adversity, the true Christian realizes and experiences the strength and substance only a life of authentic faith can produce.

Section Two: *Some Advice to Those Who Believe*

I have already addressed my observations on what might be called the general faulty thinking of the majority of professed Christians in our day. My focus was on the misunderstanding or rejection of the way Christ makes it possible for us to have a relationship with God and on the transformation of the inner person that accompanies such a relationship.

But if that is the primary problem with the state of faith in our country, there is a second that follows immediately behind. This is a problem that doesn't afflict cultural Christians who do not possess what I have called authentic faith. This is a problem that is particularly problematic for those who legitimately have received Christ and believe all that the Bible teaches. Their belief system is intact, but their lives do not bear the evidence that they have actually had a real encounter with Christ. They regard their faith as something that has been taken care of and then proceed to live as if Christ were not really their Lord. True Christian grace has become cheap grace. They have affirmed and repented from sin. They have some level of desire for holiness. But they take the path of least resistance in their approach to Christian living. They neglect a vigilant and zealous pursuit of God's will for their lives. They practice some resistance to sin and exercise some measure of discipline in dealing with the flaws of their character that God desires to change. But their approach to spiritual growth is not serious.

This problem is not only an issue for the men or women who have embraced Christianity. Sometimes it is the product of inadequate preaching by their pastors. These men and women are not cautioned from the pulpit of the dangers of this kind of approach to faith, and they are not taught what to do to strive against vice and cultivate virtue. So what you see in too many men and women is a genuine profession of belief in Jesus Christ and all He has done but little progress in authentic Christian living. They have become Christians without the slightest change in the way they use their time, talents or resources.

These men and women seem to have no ability to resist temptation when it comes. As if this isn't enough of a problem, at times they will put on a charade about what poor examples they are of the Christian faith. They display pseudo-humility and are proud of it! They put out this message with the hope that the response they receive will affirm just the opposite. They wear a false mask of sorrow for their sin. Often, this kind of behavior masks a secret self-complacency. If you think I am being too harsh, take a good look at your own heart and see how often even your humility and penitence flow from false and ego-centered motives. Too often the things we confess are far from the things that are the true deep sins in our lives. We are each like a murderer who confesses to an occasional problem with anger.

Let me warn those who are in this position: *You are in danger of deceiving yourselves.* Beware that you do not become *nominal Christians of another sort.*[8] There are no shortcuts to authentic spirituality. It takes all we have to give and is the main task to which we are called. We are instructed to grow in grace and add virtue to virtue. We are to bear the fruit of the Holy Spirit living in us and through us. When these qualities are lacking in a person's life, it might be worth it for that person to take a hard look at whether there has really been a life-changing encounter with Jesus Christ. In other words, maybe that person is not a Christian at all. It is not comfortable to address these issues, but what is the world to think when those who claim to know Christ have no different attitude toward the pursuit of wealth or ambition, or have the same desire for ostentation, that is found among the majority of humanity? They become stumbling blocks for those who look at them as examples and come to the conclusion that Christianity is a sham.

If you are serious about being a follower of Jesus Christ, keep a close watch over your behavior and your heart. Strive to learn how to overcome the obstacles you tackle on your way to spiritual maturity. Learn from those who have successfully gone before you. Read good books by men and women who have lived the faith they profess. Seek to learn the way they utilized the resources God has provided to win the battle. Study your own life. Learn where you are vulnerable. The lessons you learn about the human heart—particularly your own—will serve you well. Those lessons will help you avoid opportunities to do the wrong thing and will create true humility in your life. Careful observation and study will help produce the kind of attitude and spiritual sensitivity that is essential for you to become the person God designed you to be. It is a task that requires great diligence, but only this kind of effort will succeed. When you do, God will be glorified and you will be blessed.

Section Three: *Brief Comments to Various Kinds of Skeptics*

There is another class of men and women in this country that is growing at an alarming rate. These are the absolute unbelievers that have no interest at all in what this book is addressing. Because of my concern for them, I would like to ask them a question: If they believe that Christianity is not true, is it not at least worth taking a close look at? After all, it has been embraced, often as a result of careful examination, by some of the greatest minds of our times. Such great thinkers as Bacon, Milton, Locke, Newton and a great many others, who have carefully thought through these issues, have embraced the true Christian faith. This does not even count those who have chosen the clergy as their profession, some of whom are the most astute thinkers I know.

Can the skeptics say, with all honesty, that they have carefully examined the evidences of the faith? Have they thought all this through with the seriousness and diligence required of such an important subject? In my own investigations, I have found that unbelief is rarely a matter of examining the evidence and reaching a negative verdict. It is usually the outcome of a life that is careless and irreligious. It is usually much more of a moral issue than an intellectual one. Some people do not want to believe, even if the bulk of the evidence supports the truth of the faith.

Think about what happens to many young people who are raised with all the benefits of prosperous parents who are cultural Christians themselves. As children, they are taken to church, where they hear the parts of the Christian message that their particular church embraces. Although it is rare in our times, maybe they even receive some measure of religious instruction at home. Eventually, they leave home and launch out into the world. Some go to work; some go to college. They face temptations that they have not faced before and give in to them. Their lives might get out of control with the use of alcohol, and they might give in to sexual indulgence. At the least, they never read the Bible or make any attempt to develop a spiritual life. Most don't even attempt to take what knowledge is at their disposal and form their own beliefs and convictions. They don't learn to think.

Maybe they travel to a foreign country. Things are even worse there. They begin to embrace the ideas to which they are exposed. By the time they return home, they are further away from faith than before. Along with their previous frivolous way of life, they now begin to be consumed with the demands of making a living in the workplace and the desire for a career and success. Most of what they hear about Christianity is in a negative context. If they go to church at all, they hear things that either make no sense to them or that they find offensive to the way they live. They have no grasp of the Bible to compare with what they hear.

The result is an attitude toward Christianity that is not only negative but also one that is rooted in a faulty sense of intellectual superiority. The young also have a way of seeing right through the charade of those who profess the faith but don't live the life. What began as a vague, almost imperceptible doubt soon grows. By slow and steady degrees, the doubt becomes more fixed in their minds. In a twisted kind of way, the young men and women begin to hope their doubt is well founded. Any reason that reinforces it is welcomed. Doubt becomes greater, not based on evidence, but merely by dwelling in the mind. Ultimately, doubt overtakes all resistance and controls the mind in matters of faith. This is certainly not always how it goes, but in general you could think of this scenario as the genesis of unbelief. This is not always the process, but generally speaking, it is the natural history of skepticism. If you have carefully observed someone you know drifting into unbelief, you have probably seen something like this occur.

This has also been the theme of those who have written of their unbelief. It is interesting to read how many of these individuals describe their own lives. It is not unusual for them to speak of some time in their life when they gave some sort of intellectual assent to Christian faith. Often, this was when they were children, and merely refers to an inherited religion. What happened to move them to their new understanding that in their opinion is more enlightened? Was it some traumatic event? Was it the conclusion of some extensive research into the facts of Christianity?

Usually, these had no part in their decision. What you will find instead is that they spent many years living in a morally careless way without any regard for the true principles of authentic faith. They lived these years in relationship with others who lived the same way. They became unbelievers. Ironically, if some of these individuals turn their thinking around and become believers, it is usually by a process much more rational and careful than the process by which they embraced unbelief. They awaken to reflection. Reflection leads to investigation. And investigation leads to belief.

If this is how skepticism develops, then it would appear that unbelief is much more a matter of prejudice against Christian faith than intellectual rejection of what it believes and teaches. It is a matter of morality, not intellect. What is true of individuals is also true of cultures. Where you find a society that is marked by unbelief, you will find that it was not the product of careful investigation that led to such a mass rejection. Instead, it is often the product of a culture in which morality has been allowed to decline over a great many years. Belief declines as morals decline. Unbelief in the masses reinforces itself in the individual. Material prosperity further enhances the process.

It would seem that an unbiased look at unbelief would lead to the conclusion that it is irrational and not based on fact. Ironically, it is the opponents of Christianity who usually accuse those who believe of irrational belief based on prejudice in favor of the Christian faith. The truth appears to be that the opposite is in fact the case. It is unbelief that is based on unexamined prejudice.

In our own time, the decline of authentic faith is not the result of careful study of the writers who argue against Christianity. It is far more the product of the progress of luxury and the decline of morality. When skeptical writers do address the subject, it is usually from the point of view of sarcasm and negative wit. Their prejudices find fruitful soil in the weak minds of their readers and the faulty thinking of cultural Christians. Their sarcasm is often pointed at dimensions of faith that they have distorted in their writings to make their points. It is therefore accurate to conclude that unbelief *is in general a disease of the heart more than of the understanding.*[9]

If true Christian faith were attacked only by reason and logical argument, it would have little to fear. The philosophers and critics that have attempted this have largely been forgotten. Their names can only be found in other works that have preserved their writings from oblivion.

The same might be said of those who have abandoned orthodox Christian belief for some watered down version of true Christianity.[10] On the way from authentic faith to absolute unbelief, some have stopped at the halfway house of liberal theology. They have embraced some new religion that denies all the foundational theology of the Christian faith while still creating an illusion of religiosity. Such alternative systems often speak of the love of God and the need to practice morality, but they have gutted the faith of the theological foundations that make such actions possible. Ironically, when the lives of those who hold to these alternative systems are examined, they rarely are examples of high morality. The very reason many have turned to such religions is that they have found the truths and demands of authentic faith to be in conflict with their own lives. They are looking for a way to appear to be good without changing their behavior in the least.

When some different religious system is embraced with a degree of thoughtfulness, it is usually explained as a way of addressing the "obvious problems" with historic Christian belief. A careful assessment of these arguments will often reveal that they are targeted against issues or preconceptions that are not in fact part of the Christian faith at all. I do not intend to go into all these arguments, but I would like to point out that what these alternative religious systems do have on their side is the fact that they take the offensive against authentic Christianity. They use what they describe as powerful arguments against orthodoxy and the basic teachings of Christianity. They call men and women to abandon such things. Of course, what you will find if you examine the issues carefully is that the alternative system suggested is filled with many more problems than the original system of Christian faith it is attacking. It seems that the rational thing for any person weighing such matters to do would be to compare the "problems" of historic Christianity with the problems of these newly invented religions.

The primary beliefs of every new religion should be exposed to the same scrutiny to which historic faith is being exposed. Then, all considerations should be carefully balanced and a sound decision made. Of course, such is not usually the case. The evidence suggests that part of the approach of these new religions is to keep their adherents and potential proselytes from doing this very thing. If the tables were turned and the alternative belief systems were put on the spot, attacked both by arguments that challenged the system directly or indirectly by demonstrating the superiority of the Christian system, the new religions would not be capable of holding their ground.

In short, there are no shortcuts to spirituality. If you are going to reject Christianity on the basis that its belief system is unsound, you will find no middle ground between orthodoxy and unbelief that makes any more sense. It would be good if those who find themselves defending historic, orthodox Christian faith took such an approach to these things. By pushing these other systems to their logical conclusions, any individual who is on the fence might be led to understand that apart from authentic faith, atheism is the only logical alternative.

There is yet another group of men and women who have not rejected Christianity in deference to some other system. These individuals have attempted to dilute Christianity in such a way that they can still be in the camp with those who embrace orthodoxy, but not by embracing the whole truth. I probably don't need to point out that this attempt is also highly irrational. It usually is characterized by someone who is willing to embrace parts of the faith but who finds it necessary, in his or her own case, to reject those parts he or she finds inconvenient. These people occupy a kind of spiritual neutral zone. They have a sense that there is some truth in the claims of Christianity, but they reject the idea that everything its more committed followers claim to be the truth can really be so. They might believe in life after death, but they are hoping that things might not go so seriously when it is time for them to be evaluated. Although they might reject every main doctrine of historic Christian faith, they still see no problem with identifying themselves as Christians. They certainly would not view themselves in the same category as unbelievers, even though they reject the very truths that have given unbelief its name. The idea that they might be in spiritual danger does not cross their minds.

These men and women need to be reminded that there is no middle way. If they can be pointed to the Bible and not reject its authority, they might discover that there are no grounds for their position. They also might discover that the position they have taken is an insult to God and the work of Jesus Christ. They are attempting to get to God on their own terms. That is very risky business. In the words of the writer of Hebrews, "How shall we escape if we ignore such a great salvation?" (Heb. 2:3). I think it would be safe to say that these "half-believers," or should I say "half-unbelievers," are in worse shape than the outright skeptics. They have already admitted that the Bible might be true and that all Christ did actually happened. But they have not taken advantage of their position and pursued the truth to its logical conclusion. Of course, that is exactly why they have chosen this halfway belief.

We live at a time when there is no excuse for living in spiritual ignorance. Never before in all of human history have we had at our disposal more evidence in favor of the truth of Christianity. God, in His providence, has provided amazing resources for investigating the claims of Christ. He has also raised up a new breed of scholar who is willing and able to take on the most erudite of unbelievers in apologetic encounters. Great thinkers of our time have left behind accounts of their conversions from unbelief to Christian commitment. The time is long gone when critics can allege that the historic evidence does not support the existence and claims of Christ. The strength of this argument was one of ignorance. The weight of modern scholarship has exerted its force against many of the old objections.

It is hard to be an intelligent and informed unbeliever these days. Unfortunately for those who take such a position, what they believe or don't believe does not change one thing, except their own eternal destiny. This is what is at stake. How sad it will be on the day they discover, too late, the reality of all they have rejected. May God, in His mercy, awaken them before it is too late, and may they respond with repentance and true faith.

Section Four: *Advice for Those Who Possess Authentic Faith*

For those of you who possess authentic faith in Jesus Christ and are committed to the historic teachings of the Bible, a great deal of what I have written already has application for your lives. As both research and experience have demonstrated, you are very important members of contemporary culture. Even though that has been the case throughout the history of Christianity, I believe it could be said that never has our culture needed you more than it does today. I encourage you to take your role in society with a great deal of serious consideration.

The roles you play are crucial. All the research on the subject and all the anecdotal evidence point to the fact that standards of morality and religious faith are on the decline abroad, even more than here in our country. Still, the great concern I have is for the alarming rate that unbelief and evil are growing right here at home. Something must be done to combat this growing trend. If change is to come, it must start with true Christians living out their faith. It is imperative that men and women of authentic faith live out their relationship with Christ in such a way that the Church in our country again regains the respect of the culture and the allegiance of its membership. It is going to take passion to change things, and only those who truly believe are capable of having it. True believers are going to have to go the distance.

You must strive with all you have and with true sincerity to make a difference in this country. By your life and words you must put to silence the voices of ignorant critics of the faith. Be bold to proclaim the name of Christ in this time when many who call themselves Christian are ashamed to speak the name. You may have a greater impact on this nation than that of any politician if you make it your goal to help restore the influence of Christian faith and raise the standard of our nation's morality.

Get going. Be useful, generous, moderate and self-denying in your manner of life. Treat the lack of positive action on your part as sin. If God chooses to bless you with material prosperity, don't use it on the absurd task of keeping up with the current trends and fads. By using your money modestly and without display, show that you are not a slave to fashion. Be an example of someone who uses his or her wealth for purposes that are more important than showing off or making a big impression. Demonstrate through the way you live that worldly things are not even close to the value of heavenly things. Show that you have riches that have nothing to do with material possessions and which material wealth can never acquire. Seek to form friendships with men and women of other denominations who hold to the essentials of the faith, even if they differ from you in the non-essentials. Work together with them on this great task. Pray faithfully that God might give you good success and that once again this nation might know the joy of living with a vital faith.

We live in difficult times. Pray for this nation. We have all the marks of a declining civilization. Pray that the God who hears and answers the prayers of His people might intervene on behalf of our country and bring a spiritual renewal that might save the nation. People of unbelief might think you are kidding yourself to think that prayer can make a difference. They might think you are like some superstitious pagan who depends on God because you are weak. They might compare you to those who really are a bit out of touch.[11] The fact is that God cares for the nations in which His servants live and serve Him. He favors and blesses the land of the righteous (see Prov. 3:33).

I find it necessary to affirm that the problems we face nationally and internationally are *a direct result of the decline of faith and morality in our nation. My only hope of a prosperous future for this country rests not on the size and firepower of our military, nor on the wisdom of its leaders, nor on the sprit of her people, but only on the love and obedience of the people who name themselves after Christ, that their prayers might be heard and for the sake of these, God might look upon us with favor.*[12]

Would all who read this book and live with authentic faith in Jesus Christ pray for the work that those in this country of like-mindedness need to accomplish. Pray for us. God can use anything. I would be deeply grateful if this book motivates someone who is simply a cultural Christian to take a good look at his or her faith, or someone who possesses authentic faith to strive to become more effective in the expression of what he or she believes.

I may not seem like the right person to have taken on the task of writing such a book, and I might be accused of presumption and arrogance for taking on the role of a spiritual teacher. However, I simply have attempted to execute the proper responsibilities that accompany my office in the government—to take a hard look at and evaluate the state of religion and morals in our country. I also believe it is the job of a real patriot to seek to halt their decline and promote their revival. I hope you will give me the benefit of the doubt and know that I have written what I have written both to accomplish what I view to be an act of service to my country and to discharge what I believe to be a solemn responsibility to my friends and countrymen.

I am genuinely concerned for the welfare of all humanity. I can only hope and wish that while much of the modern world has embraced a false philosophy of life and rejected the message of the gospel, and while unbelief and the morality that accompanies it have grown to such an extent that immorality and vice prevail without restraint, this land might yet become a sanctuary—a place of faith and piety—where the blessings of true Christianity might still be enjoyed. I pray that this might be a land where the name of Jesus Christ would still be honored and that we might be a place where the rest of the world can look and see the blessings of faithfully following Christ. I pray that if God might so ordain, our nation will be one that spreads to neighboring countries and the world at large the truth and benefits that come to any nation whose citizens confess and practice lives of authentic faith.

Notes

1. As in previous chapters, Wilberforce does not give a title to this section.
2. This is an exact quote from Wilberforce, including italics.
3. Italics by Wilberforce.
4. Italics by Wilberforce.

5. Horace, *Ars Poetica*, lines 166-168.
6. Cicero, *De Senectute*, 23:85.
7. I borrowed this expression from C. S. Lewis, *The Last Battle* (New York: Collier Books, 1972), p. 176. It captures what Wilberforce is saying here.
8. Italics by Wilberforce.
9. Italics by Wilberforce.
10. Wilberforce is specifically referring to the Unitarianism of his time, which at one point he himself embraced before "Great Change."
11. Wilberforce is here referring to some superstitious inhabitants of Sicily who, at this time, used idols to attempt to stop Mount Aetna from blowing its top.
12. Italics by Wilberforce.

Recommended Bibliography

Compiled by Kevin Belmonte

Anstey, Roger. *The Atlantic Slave Trade and British Abolition, 1760-1810*. Atlantic Highlands, NJ: Humanities Press, 1975.

Belmonte, Kevin. *Hero for Humanity: A Biography of William Wilberforce*. Colorado Springs, CO: NavPress, 2002.

———. "William Wilberforce." Essay in the anthology, *Building a Healthy Culture: Strategies for an American Renaissance*, edited by Don Eberly, pp. 159-180. Grand Rapids, MI: W. B. Eerdmans Pub. Company, 2001.

Coupland, Sir Reginald. *Wilberforce: A Narrative*. Oxford: Oxford University Press, 1923.

Furneaux, Robin. *William Wilberforce*. London: Hamish Hamilton, 1974.

Piper, John. *The Roots of Endurance: Invincible Perseverance in the Lives of John Newton, Charles Simeon, and William Wilberforce*. The Swans Are Not Silent series, bk. 3. Wheaton, IL: Crossway Books, 2002.

Pollock, John. *Wilberforce*. London: John Constable, 1977.

Pura, Murray. *Vital Christianity: The Life and Spirituality of William Wilberforce*. Toronto, Canada: Clements Publishing, 2002.

About the Author

Dr. Bob Beltz is a popular writer, speaker and film producer. Currently, he oversees film development for the Anschutz Corporation, parent company of the Anschutz Film Group and Walden Media (*Holes, Because of Winn-Dixie, The Lion, the Witch and the Wardrobe*), and he produced the Walden-Media film about William Wilberforce's life titled *Amazing Grace*. Formerly, Beltz spent 20 years in ministry, first as founding and teaching pastor of Cherry Hills Community Church in Denver, Colorado, and then as senior pastor of High Street Community Church in Santa Cruz, California. Beltz is a graduate of Denver Seminary where he earned both his Master of Arts and Doctor of Ministry degrees. He is the author of several books, including *Somewhere Fast* and *Becoming a Man of Prayer*. Bob's wife of more than 30 years, Allison, is a religious liberty and human rights advocate, and together their work with the Dalits (Untouchables) of India is a living example of all Wilberforce stood for. When not writing, speaking or making movies, Bob can usually be seen heading into the mountains of Colorado on his Harley-Davidson with a group of cultural infidels.

More Ways to Seek Justice

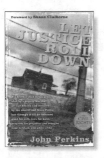

The Justice God Is Seeking
Responding to the Heart of God
Through Compassionate Worship
David Ruis
ISBN 08307.41976

Practitioners
Voices Within the Emerging
Church
Greg Russinger and *Alex Field,*
General Editors
ISBN 08307.38088

Let Justice Roll Down
A Civil Rights Classic
John Perkins
ISBN 08307.43073

**Changing the World
Through Kindness**
Living a Life That Will
Change Your Family, Your
City—and
Eventually the World
Steve Sjogren
ISBN 08307.36727

Hands & Feet
Inspiring Stories and
Firsthand Accounts of
God Changing Lives
Audio Adrenaline
ISBN 08307.39327

**Everybody Wants to
Change the World**
Practical Ideas for Social
Justice
Tony Campolo
ISBN 08307.42832

sub-merge
Living Deep in a Shallow
World: Service, Justice and
Contemplation Among
the World's Poor
John B. Hayes
ISBN 08307.43065